**What Would Jesus Ask You Today?**
by John W. Stanko


Note: all bold text in Bible quotations are author's emphasis.

ISBN 978-1-63360-015-7
For Worldwide Distribution
Printed in the U.S.A.

Urban Press
P.O. Box 8882
Pittsburgh, PA 15221-0882
412.646.2780

# Introduction

The year was 2007 and I ran across a quote from a motivational speaker that said, "Quality questions lead to a quality life." I pondered that statement for a while and determined that it was true. For the believer, it is actually another way of "seeking the Lord." For what else would you seek the Lord for except answers. And what requires answers but, you got it, questions!

Shortly after discovering this quote, I began reading the gospels and, since questions were on my mind, I noticed, probably for the first time, that Jesus asked a lot of questions. When I started looking for them, I found 156 or so in all the gospels, but of course that number includes questions repeated in more than one gospel. Still that is a lot of questions! After I searched, I copied and pasted all the gospel questions into one document and put it on my website where people could access them and meditate or pray about them. I got some good feedback and everyone said what I pointed out: They had not noticed how many questions Jesus asked in the course of His teaching.

Then one day I noticed this exchange between Jesus and a man in the context of questions in Matthew 19:16-21:

> Just then a man came up to Jesus and asked, "Teacher, what good thing must I do to get eternal life?" "Why do you ask me about what is good?" Jesus replied. "There is only One who is good. If you want to enter life, keep the commandments." "Which ones?" he inquired. Jesus replied, "'You shall not murder, you shall not commit adultery, you shall not steal, you shall not give false tes-timony, honor your father and mother,' and 'love your neighbor as yourself.'" "All these I have kept," the young man said. "What do I still lack?" Jesus answered, "If you want to be perfect, go, sell your possessions and give to the poor, and you will have treasure in heaven. Then come, follow me."

Notice the progression of insight this man received in this instance. Why didn't Jesus tell him to sell his possessions at the start of the conversation? Probably because the man didn't ask! The man kept asking and Jesus kept giving him more insight. This indicates that when you ask God quality questions you get quality answers; although they may not be the answers you want to hear. But that's what seeking the

Lord with quality questions is all about.

The final step in producing the daily devotional you hold in your hand or read on your computer or e-reader occurred in November, 2011. I was finishing up a devotional focusing on a daily verse from Proverbs. I asked this question as I was seeking wisdom for my next devotional: "I wonder if I could pose a question every day from Scripture, write some devotional material and ask my own questions to help the reader grasp how to use that question to get quality answers in 2012?"

I decided the answer was "Yes!", so I began on January 1, 2012 to post a daily devotional using a question from the Bible, titling the series, "What Would Jesus Ask You Today?" I knew there was a line of products and jewelry one time with the theme "What Would Jesus Do (WWJD)?", and a series of health books entitled, "What Would Jesus Eat?" I thought "What Would Jesus Ask You Today?" fit right in with those titles.

Remember, however, that I said the gospels had 156 questions and, of course, there are 366 days in a leap year. What was I going to do after I exhausted those questions? It was a simple answer: I would look in the epistles, then Psalms, then Proverbs and finally the rest of the Old Testament to find questions. While Jesus did not specifically ask those questions, they do come from the inspired Word of God and since Jesus is referred to as the Word in John's gospel, I didn't think it too much of a stretch to include those questions from the Old Testament and epistles as if Jesus was actually asking them.

What you see are the results of my daily efforts to pose a quality question and help you get a quality answer. I am especially pleased that I have included all 66 books of the Bible in this devotional, drawing from the questions or the cross references to include them all. I like this because the Bible is so interconnected that I always love to find another reference con-cerning the topic at hand.

At the end of this book is a listing of all verses utilized by book of the Bible, in case you are looking for a particular one. I used the list to make sure I did not duplicate any verses, although there are a few duplicates that seemed right to use more than once. And since some of Jesus' questions are repeated in the gospels, I do include those, but tried to write something different any time I repeated a question.

There you have the basic layout and history behind this devotional. I hope you will find it as stimulating and rewarding as many did who followed it using my blog, my Facebook page or my twitter account. If you have some insight or thoughts to share, you can write me at johnstanko@gmail.com. And you can access my other Bible studies from on my website at www. stankobiblestudies.com. My other devotionals in print are all available through www.amazon.com and several of my books are in the Kindle format so you can download them.

In a church I once attended, we would sing an old hymn before the preaching of God's word. It went like this:

Bless Thy word unto our hearts and glorify Thy name
Bless Thy word unto our hearts and glorify Thy name
Glorify Thy name, Lord, glorify Thy name
Bless Thy word unto our hearts and glorify Thy name

May the Lord bless the reading and study of His word in your life.

In His and Your Service,

John W. Stanko
Pittsburgh, PA USA
April, 2014

# What Would Jesus Ask You Today?

## January

## January 1: Flavor

*"But if the salt loses its saltiness, how can it be made salty again?" - Matthew 5:13.*

Salt was and is used to preserve or flavor food. Salt is used to represent influence for no one eats salt alone but wants it in their food. You are to be like salt, representing God in whatever situation you find yourself, influencing circumstances and people for Him. **Is your witness credible in your workplace, family, or neighborhood? In other words, is your salt still salty? What are you doing to improve situations in which you find yourself? What can you do to be more salty, making people thirsty for the Lord? Is your influence being felt wherever God chooses for you to be?** Read Colossians 4:2-6 and meditate on what it means to season your words and life with salt.

## January 2: Love Your Enemies

*"If you love those who love you, what reward will you get?" - Matthew 5:46.*

It is a godly trait to love those who are unloving or unlovely to you, yet that is exactly what God does. **Do you have someone in your life who is not worthy of your love? Perhaps you even have an enemy of sorts?** Then determine today to love them anyway. What's more, Jesus implied that there is a reward in doing so! Read Matthew 5:44-45 to understand the context of what Jesus was asking you to do.

## January 3: Priorities

*"Is not life more important than food, and the body more important than clothes?" - Matthew 6:25.*

This question tries to help you establish priorities. The context also urges you not to worry about the necessities of life, for the Lord is capable of providing while you focus on the most important thing, which is doing the will of God! **Are you consumed with worry these days? Are your priorities out of order?** If so, read Matthew 6:33-34 and do what Jesus directs.

## January 4: Courage

*"You of little faith, why are you so afraid?"*
*- Matthew 8:26.*

Our parents Adam and Eve were afraid and hid from God after they sinned. You have inherited their propensity for fear and shame. **Where is fear crippling your ability to serve the Lord? Where is it keeping you from fulfilling your purpose or dreams?** Someone once said that courage is not the absence of fear but rather learning to function in the midst of it. Read Deuteronomy 31:6 and then take action today that will help you overcome any fear that hinders you and the achievement of your purpose and dreams.

## January 5: Doubt

*"Why did you doubt?" - Matthew 14:31.*

God has been faithful to you throughout your life and you have no reason to believe that will change. Yet it is so easy to doubt when things don't go as planned or when answers to problems are not forthcoming. What's more, God is seldom early but He is always on time, which can cause you to doubt along the way. **Are you living in doubt or faith? Are you asking in faith or holding back because you don't want to be disappointed?** Read what James said in James 1:5-8 about asking for and receiving wisdom and apply that principle to your life in as many areas as possible.

## January 6: Unbelief

*"Do you believe I am able to do this?" - Matthew 9:28.*

You may know God has the power to do something for someone, but **do you believe He will do it for you, whatever the "it" represents?** Jesus posed this question to two blind men who asked to be healed and they answered an emphatic yes! Jesus went on to heal them. Ask yourself this question about some need or goal you have, and don't be afraid to face your unbelief. Just don't be content to stay there. Read what the father said to Jesus when asked if he had faith in Mark 9:23-25 and then be honest with the Lord. **Where are you afraid to admit your unbelief? Since fear is the enemy of faith, what are you afraid of that is keeping you from expressing faith?**

## January 7: Knowledge

*"Who do you say I am?" - Matthew 16:15.*

Jesus asked Peter this question and Peter gave the correct answer. In a sense Jesus asks everyone this question. The answer each gives has eternal implications. **How do you answer this question? If you know Him, are you growing in your knowledge of who He is and His requirements for you?** You can only do that by reading His word and having regular contact with His people. Read Paul's growth goals for you in Philippians 1:9-11 and then work to be able to answer today's important question.

## January 8: Awareness

*"What do you think?" - Matthew 18:12.*

Jesus asked this question often, so we will encounter it regularly throughout this study. It is important that we are self-aware and recognize and examine what is going on inside our minds and hearts. **Are you worried, anxious, hesitant, happy, or sad? Are you regularly thinking about doing something or going somewhere, but dismiss it as nonsense?** While reflecting on your emotions and thoughts, it is also necessary to think about the things of God and what He requires of you, your life, and your gifts. Notice after Paul's vision in Acts 16:6-10 that the ministry team "concluded" they were to go to Macedonia. Don't be afraid to evaluate your circumstances, your heart and mind, and your behavior, and come to conclusions consistent with the evidence of where you are spiritually and why you are there--and where you need to go.

## January 9: Pay Attention

*"Do you see all these things?" - Matthew 24:2.*

**Did you ever notice that you can pass things regularly and not really see or notice them because they have no value to or meaning for you?** Sometimes you can be preoccupied with yourself or not paying attention, and can then can easily pass by someone who is hurting, worried, or angry. Make an effort today to "read" the people around you and then be willing and available to help them according to their need. For an example of this dynamic, read 2 Kings 4:25-27 and see how the prophet went out of his way to meet the widow's need once God opened his eyes to see it. Then go do the same.

## January 10: Relevance

*"To what can I compare this generation?"*
*- Matthew 11:16.*

Jesus did not seek to distance Himself from His generation, but looked for ways to understand and reach it. He asks you to do the same, otherwise you will become irrelevant and your message about Him will fall on deaf ears. **Do you study current trends to understand this generation's spiritual problems? What are you doing to engage this generation in order to present the gospel message?** Read what Jesus said about being in, but not of, the world in John 17:15-18, and then do what you must to be relevant today.

## January 11: God Speaks

*"Have you not read what God said to you, 'I am the God of*

*Abraham, the God of Isaac, and the God of Jacob?'"*
*- Matthew 22:31-32.*

Jesus acknowledged that God speaks to you through His Word. It is His self-revelation to mankind, and you, and all men must consider His Word to be true. That being said, **how much time do you spend reading the Bible to learn God's thoughts and direction for you? You are just a few days into a new year. Are you keeping your resolution to spend more time in the Word?** Read what the psalmist wrote in Psalm 119:9-16 to grasp why and how to study the Word.

## January 12: Your Focus

*"How many loaves do you have?" - Matthew 15:34.*

Faith never requires you to ignore your current reality. It does require that you not make it your focus. Instead you are to make God's goodness and promises your focus. An excellent example of this is Abraham, who fully recognized the reality of his age but did not waver in his faith that God would give him a child (see Romans 4:18-25). **Have you allowed your current lack or need to overwhelm your faith? Have you lost sight of the fact that God can take your "few loaves" and multiply them into many?**

## January 13: Salvation

*"How will you escape being condemned to hell?"*
*- Matthew 23:33.*

Of course there is only one way to avoid the destiny Jesus mentioned and that is to put one's faith in the Lord Jesus Christ to forgive sins and grant eternal life. For all who do that, He promises that not one will be lost (see John 17:11-12). For those who do not, there is no other name under heaven by which men can be saved (see Acts 4:12). **Have you put your faith in Christ? Are you proclaiming the message of salvation to others who don't know? Are you convinced Jesus is the only way to obtain a right-standing with God?**

# January 14: Heart's Desire

*"What is it you want?" - Matthew 20:21.*

Many are wary of what is in their heart, having been conditioned to think that their heart is evil. Yet the Spirit is in you to give you the mind of Christ, so at some point you must learn to trust His work in you. **Are you afraid of what is in your heart? Then how can you explain Psalm 37:4, where God promises to give you the desires of your heart?** Get past your fears and hangups and learn to articulate clearly what it is that you want the Lord to do for you or accomplish through you.

# January 15: Traditions

*"And why do you break the command of God for the sake of your tradition?" - Matthew 15:3.*

The commands of God are found in the Word of God and those commands are your guides of life and behavior. Nothing is to supersede those commands, yet the prevailing culture works to counteract those commands. For instance, culture wants you sometimes to work on Sunday but the Word directs you to worship. **Are there any areas in your life where you have allowed culture or tradition to contradict God's clear commands for you?** Read what Paul wrote about this in Colossians 2:16-23 and ask yourself the same question again.

# January 16: God's Patience

*"How long shall I stay with you?*
*How long shall I put up with you?" - Matthew 17:17.*

God's patience is not endless, although He is long-suffering, not wishing that any perish but that all will come to the truth. Don't mistake God's tolerance, however, for acceptance or approval of your attitudes or behaviors. Paul wrote in Romans 2:4 that God's kindness is intended to lead you to repentance, and Psalm 50:21 warns, "When you did these things and I kept silent, you thought I was exactly like you. But I now arraign you and set my accusations before you." **Are you assuming God approves of your thoughts and actions? Are there any attitudes or behaviors of which you need to repent today?** Don't respond too quickly, but ask God to help you see clearly.

## January 17: Mind Your Business

*"Why do you look at the speck of sawdust in your brother's eye and pay no attention to the plank in your own eye?" - Luke 6:41.*

Don't be too anxious to help others with their problems unless you are willing to deal with your own first and foremost. What's more, the image in today's verse indicates that you can't really see clearly to help others unless you are addressing your own issues. **Do you have a tendency to be critical of others yet excuse your own faults and weaknesses?** Paul spoke about confronting and helping others while being mindful of yourself in Galatians 6:1-5.

## January 18: History

*"Do you still have no faith?" - Mark 4:40.*

Think about your history in the Lord. **Has He ever failed you? Then why are you so worried about tomorrow?** God has given you no reason to doubt Him or His ability to care for you and yours. As an example of what can happen to people who saw God's work but panicked and had no faith, consider the Israelites who went in to spy out the land and brought back a negative report in Numbers 13:26-14:9. Then determine by God's grace not to be like them.

# January 19: Hindrances

*"Do you want to get well?" - John 5:6.*

It is interesting that Jesus would ask a sick person if he wanted to get better. Sometimes you can become attached or addicted to the drama or problems in your life. **Do you want to make progress in your life?** Then maybe you need to change your habits, friends, diet or routine, or else you will never "get well." Read James 4:4 and see if there are things in life that are preventing God's blessings from getting through to you.

# January 20: Shine!

*"Do you bring in a lamp to put it under a bowl or a bed?" - Mark 4:21.*

The answer to this question is an obvious no, yet that may be what you are doing if you don't let the light of God's love in your life shine before others. This means to show forth the fullness of who He made you to be where your creativity and purpose are concerned. You are not to play small if God has given you a big gift capable of touching and blessing many people. **What are you doing to "broadcast" God's goodness to you? Are you allowing your light to shine before men and women of darkness? When is the last time you gave a testimony to anyone of God's work in your life? Are you doing all you can to express your creativity so others can enjoy it?** Read Jesus' words in Matthew 5:14-16 and don't be afraid to let your light shine.

# January 21: No Substitute

*"Or what can a man give in exchange for his soul?" - Matthew 16:26.*

The answer to this question is "nothing," but that doesn't stop men and women from trying to find things to fill the void that only God can fill. John Calvin said that man's heart is an idol factory, constantly creating things to worship instead of the living God. **Are you looking**

**for satisfaction or even salvation in things other than the Lord, things like relationships, status, money, work or even good deeds?** Read Jesus' parable in Luke 12:16-21 and see if you are like the man described in any way.

## January 22: Suffering

*"Can you drink the cup I am going to drink?" - Matthew 20:22.*

Jesus spent the latter part of His ministry warning His disciples about His coming suffering, death, and resurrection. The cup Jesus was referring to in this verse was and is the cup of suffering, and you will drink of it, just like He did. Sometimes you suffer for the things you have done, sometimes for a stand you take for Him, and sometimes due to the acts of others you love who hurt you—either on purpose or inadvertently. **Where is the cause for your suffering at this point in your life? Can you see that God is using it for His purpose to work something in your life (or remove something from your life)? Can you praise Him in the midst of the pain?** Read 1 Peter 4, which has a lot to say about suffering and how to respond in it.

## January 23: Need

*"Who touched me?" Jesus asked - Luke 8:45.*

The answer is the woman who needed healing. She pressed through a crowd and had faith to touch the hem of Jesus' garment because she knew her need for Him. **Are you earnestly seeking the Lord? Are you aware of your need?** If not, then you will go about your business. If you do, then you will urgently seek Him. Read Isaiah 55:6 and Psalm 27:8 and then seek to 'touch' the Lord according to your area of need.

## January 24: What Matters Most

*"Do you see all these great buildings?" - Mark 13:2*

Man has been busy building since the Tower of Babel in Genesis 11:1-9. Yet the Lord is busy with other things: building His church and extending His kingdom. **Are your priorities the same as His?** Don't invest time in things that will last for a while and then pass away. Put your money and effort into what matters most, and God will work with you and reward you. Read Psalm 146:1-5 and meditate on its message.

## January 25: Be a Blessing

*"Why are you bothering this woman?" - Matthew 26:10.*

The Bible is full of directives on how to treat others, but selfishness can prevent you from obeying. You are to be a blessing to others and not bothersome; look for chances to give rather than receive; encourage and not gossip or slander; serve and meet the needs of others and not just look after yourself. **What is keeping you from loving others as the gospel demands?** Read a good overview of how to treat others in Colossians 3:12-17 and then go do it.

## January 26: Your Temper

*"'What are you arguing with them about?' he asked." - Mark 9:16.*

It is common to say that someone "lost" their temper, but in some ways they found" it when they get into a heated argument or when someone does them wrong. If this is a regular occurrence, then someone is said to have an anger "problem." In today's verse, Jesus inquired as to the source of the argument among the disciples. An argument is a battle to prove that someone is right and someone else is wrong, when both may be wrong or partially right. **Are you prone to argue? Would you or others say you have an anger issue? Why is being right so important? Why hurt someone you love or offend an acquaintance just to be "right" or to retaliate for being wronged?** There are many verses that speak to controlling anger, but for today read and 1 Timothy 2:8 and then confront any areas of anger in your heart.

# January 27: The Kingdom

*"What shall we say the kingdom of God is like, or what parable shall we use to describe it?" - Mark 4:30.*

Jesus proclaimed and then taught us how to live in the kingdom of God. However, his peers were expecting a more political kingdom which often caused them to misinterpret what the Lord was preaching and teaching. He was announcing that He was the King and wasn't simply interested in saving us, but in having us live every area of life according to His commands, including relationships, finances, work, and family. **Have you thought of yourself first as a church person or a Kingdom person? Do you know what God's kingdom requirements are for you? Are you living them out?** Read Acts 14:21-22 and Romans 14:16-18 to get a basic definition of God's kingdom and then make every effort with His help to live up to its and His expectations.

# January 28: Neighbor

*"Which of these three do you think was a neighbor to the man who fell into the hands of robbers?" - Luke 10:36.*

Jesus often taught with parables and there was always one lesson to be learned. This question is at the end of the parable of the Good Samaritan and the lesson is to love your neighbor. **What are you doing to be a good neighbor to someone in need? How much are you willing to be inconvenienced to be that good neighbor? Do you even have any relationships with people who are in need so you can play some role in their relief?** Read this parable in its entirety in Luke 10:25-37 and then ask the Lord to help you apply the main point to your life today and every day.

# January 29: Continue

*"What did Moses command you?" - Mark 10:3.*

Jesus constantly referred His listeners back to God's word as their source for answers and perspective. Because He was addressing people of the Word, He assumed that they knew the Word well enough to discuss it and learn from His lessons. **Is that the case in your life? Do you know the Word? Are you growing in your understanding of it and how to apply it to life's problems and opportunities?** Paul urged Timothy to "continue" in the Word in 2 Timothy 3:14-17; you would do well to follow Paul's advice and invest time in becoming more familiar with the Word, perhaps teaching it to others as a means to learn and grow for yourself.

## January 30: Give Thanks

*"Was no one found to return and give praise to God except this foreigner?" - Luke 17:18.*

Jesus healed ten lepers, but only one returned to say thank you. What's more, Jesus noticed and commented on this fact, which meant that it was important to Him. **Are you mindful of what God has done and is doing for you? How often do you give thanks for specific things He has done?** Read Psalm 9:1 and sit down to make a list of all things for which you are grateful. Then spend some time today thanking Him for His goodness towards you.

## January 31: Expectations

*"Again he asked them, 'Who is it you want?'" - John 18:7.*

You have a God-sized hole in your life that cannot be filled with any relationship other than God. Yet often you can expect others to meet that need, which only leads to frustration and pain. **Are you currently expecting friends, spouse, children or fellow church members to do for you what only the Lord can do?** Read what Jacob said to his wife in Genesis 30:1-2 and then release anyone upon whom you have placed unrealistic expectations.

# What Would Jesus Ask You Today?

## February

## February 1: Pressured for Reasons

*"If anyone asks you, 'Why are you doing this?' tell him, 'The Lord needs it and will send it back here shortly'" - Mark 11:3.*

People will always ask you the reasons why you are doing something that doesn't make sense to them. Don't be under pressure to explain the rationale that will make sense to them. Just tell them the Lord directed you to do it and then get busy doing it! **Are you being intimidated by those closest to you who are demanding answers?** Read Acts 21:12-14 and see how Paul responded to those who questioned his actions.

## February 2: Maturity

*"You are Israel's teacher," said Jesus, "and do you not understand these things?" - John 3:10.*

As you mature in your faith, Jesus expects you to grow in your knowledge of who He is and how He works in your life and that of others. **Are you growing in your knowledge of Him so that you can explain your faith to others? Can you help them see what you have come to know?** Read Hebrews 5:11- 6:3 to learn the responsibilities of a mature believer.

## February 3: Peace

*"Do you think I came to bring peace on earth?" - Luke 12:51.*

Jesus is the Prince of Peace, but there can be no peace for those who are not right with God. Therefore, His presence, and sometimes your presence as His representative, can be the source of un-peaceful and unpleasant things for others. **Are you afraid of conflict or criticism as you represent the Lord? Are there some whom you seem to upset no matter what you do?** Jesus had the same effect on some, so you should not feel badly or alter your witness for the sake of peace. Read Hebrews 12:14 and Romans 12:18 and then seek to be a source of peace without compromising your stand for the Lord if your stand happens to stir up those who oppose righteousness.

## February 4: Obedience

*"Why do you call me, 'Lord, Lord,' and do not do what I say?" - Luke 6:46.*

Jesus places great emphasis on obedience, not just in word but in deed. To do what Jesus says, you must first know His Word. Then you must determine, by God's grace, to obey what you read, which is for the most part pretty simple. For example, the commands to be generous, love your neighbor, forgive and pray are not complicated; they are just difficult to do at times. **Where is your walk not consistent with your talk?** Read what James had to say about having faith but not following through with action in James 2:14-26.

## February 5: Worry

*"Who of you by worrying can add a single hour to his life?" - Luke 12:25.*

In other words, Jesus was asking, What possible benefit is there to worrying? Yet we engage in this practice as if fretting over something can actually change the future. And there is a physical price to worry, for it can lead to ulcers, cancer, and other physical and mental disorders that take life away rather than give it. **Are you fed up with worry? Do you see that it is not just a bad habit but rather a sin? Can you accept that you have dominion over worry by managing your thoughts and what you say to yourself when faced with something you cannot control?** If so, then make a decision to stop after you learn how to replace worry in Philippians 4:4-9.

## February 6: Seek Him

*"Why were you searching for me?" he asked - Luke 2:29.*

The fact that you are searching for God is evidence that He is searching for you, working in your life and heart to create a hunger for Him. **Are you fighting or resisting this urge to seek Him? How much energy and time are you investing in the search? What are you doing with what you discover?** Searching and seeking Him cannot be a passive effort, but requires energy and diligence on your part. Read Psalm 27:8 and let that be your motto as you commit to search for Him and seek His face with all your heart.

## February 7: Take Time

*"'Do you understand what I have done for you?' he asked them" - John 13:12.*

It's important that you take time to reflect on all that God has done for you and to express gratitude for His work and grace in your life. It helps if you take time to journal your thoughts so you can have a written record to review from time to time. **Do you have a journal? If not, why not? If so, are you faithful to record not just your thoughts about life, but also your thoughts about God?** Use Psalm 77:11-13 as a guide as you reflect on and journal about God's goodness.

## February 8: Offense

*"Jesus said to them, 'Does this offend you?'" - John 6:61.*

Things can happen that you don't expect, and they can cause you to be offended that God did not prevent them or intervene on your behalf. **Is it time that you be reminded of the great truth in Romans 8:31-39 that nothing can separate you from the love of God?** The only thing not listed in that list is "you," for you can choose to separate yourself when you think you know better than God about your welfare and future.

# February 9: Anything

*"What do you want me to do for you?" - Mark 10:36.*

Jesus asked this question of many and He is asking you today. Your answer requires that you understand your need before the Lord and His ability to do anything. Yet you can be afraid to ask because it seems too great or unbelief can cause you to ask for little or nothing at all. **What do you want the Lord to do for you today? Is there anything for which you are afraid to ask?** Read Luke 18:27 and then respond to today's question with faith.

# February 10: Invest Wisely

*"What good is it for a man to gain the whole world, and yet lose or forfeit his very self?" - Luke 9:25.*

You reap what you sow. If you sow into worldly things you will gain what the world has to offer. If you sow into God's things you will gain what He has to offer. If you gain the former, you actually lose, but if you invest in the latter, you will gain what really matters. **Where are you investing your energy, time and resources?** Jesus urged you to store up treasure where it cannot be destroyed in Luke 12:32-34. How can you best apply what He advised you to do?

# February 11: Dig Deep

*"Don't you understand this parable?" - Mark 4:13.*

Jesus taught in parables so those who were interested in the things He said would dig deeper and ask questions, trying to grasp and then apply what He meant. Perhaps He had Proverbs 25:2 in mind as one reason for His parables: "It is the glory of God to conceal a matter; to search out a matter is the glory of kings." When you invest time and effort into something, you value the results as another proverbs reminds us: "Buy the truth and do not sell it—wisdom, instruction and insight as well" (Proverbs 23:23). **Are you among those who are**

**interested in seeking the meaning of what Jesus said and did? If so, what are you doing to understand His words? What price are you willing to pay to buy His truth? What can you do to ensure you don't exchange that truth for a lie?** Of course, the best way to dig deeper is to read and study the Bible. Look at Proverbs 4:5 that reiterates your need to dig and search if you want to understand.

## February 12: Facts and Faith

*"How long has he been like this?" - Mark 9:21.*

This is what Jesus asked a father while the son was having a seizure in front of them both. Jesus was calm and composed, for He knew the power He had to help and heal, but wanted His disciples to hear the scope of the problem so their own faith could grow. Faith never requires that you ignore the facts. It simply mandates that the facts not determine what you will ask or believe God to do for you. **Where have you allowed the facts to hinder rather than activate your faith?** Read Hebrews 11:1-6 and notice that what is seen has its foundation in the unseen, and then learn to walk in faith in the invisible while not ignoring the reality of the visible.

## February 13: Work of the Lord

*"Do you see all these things?" - Matthew 24:2.*

The disciples were enamored with Jerusalem and the magnificence of the Temple because it was one of the wonders of the ancient world. Yet in spite of its engineering excellence and size, it was destined to be destroyed in a few decades, and today people visit its ruins. In fact, everything you work for is heading toward the same end. **To what or whom are you giving the best of your time, talents, and treasure? To things that are destined to pass away or to God's work and kingdom, which will never pass away?** Read 1 Corinthians 15:50-58 and then invest your best efforts in serving God and His purpose for your life.

# February 14: Remember

*"Don't you remember the five loaves for the five thousand, and how many basketfuls you gathered?" - Matthew 16:9.*

You have a history of how God has taken care of you. **Why are you worried today? Have you forgotten how He has worked in the past?** He may not have always come immediately when you called Him, but He has always come on time! Read 1 Chronicles 16:12-14, and then spend time today remembering and thanking God for His provision and grace in your life.

# February 15: Family

*"Who are my mother and my brothers?" - Mark 3:33.*

Jesus answered His own question by saying anyone who obeys the Father is part of His family. **Do you realize that you are part of God's family through Christ?** That means that you have obligations not only to the Father, but to His children. **Do you identify with His children through worship, fellowship and other ways you gather together?** Read Hebrews 10:23- 25 and then renew your commitment to be an active part of God's family.

# February 16: Faith

*"Where is your faith?" - Luke 8:25.*

**Where is your faith? Is it in your own abilities, in your company or culture?** Those are vital questions to answer, for faith in anything less than God and His word is faulty faith that is doomed to disappoint you. Take the time today to read Hebrews 11 and pick out one of the faith heroes listed thereto study to learn about and imitate their faith.

# February 17: Eyes and Ears

*"Do you have eyes but fail to see,*

*and ears but fail to hear?" - Mark 8:18.*

You don't see or hear with your eyes and ears. You see and hear with your brain and sometimes your thinking can actually block or cause you to misinterpret what is happening right in front of you. That can happen even with spiritual things. **Are you willing to ask the Lord to open your ears and eyes to see what you are unable to see and hear?** Read 2 Kings 6:8-17 to see what can happen when God opens your eyes!

## February 18: Freedom

*"How can anyone enter a strong man's house and carry off his possessions unless he first ties up the strong man?" - Matthew 12:29.*

Jesus was referring to the power of the devil under which all mankind operated until He came. Now there is a power that is able to set you free, but only if you choose freedom. **Are you applying the power of God to set you free in every area of your life, including thoughts, actions, what you watch and what you do?** Read Acts 10:37-38 and then ask if that same dynamic is present in your own relationship with Jesus.

## February 19: Work It Out

*"Why are you thinking these things in your hearts?" - Luke 5:22.*

It is not enough to change your external behavior; you must change at the heart level because you may be smiling while harboring all kinds of hidden thoughts and attitudes in your heart that lead to bitterness, anger, and even hatred. What's more, your thoughts are not beyond your control, although you may have to work diligently to change your thinking that you have developed over a long period of time. **Do you desire to have God change you on the inside? Are you willing to cooperate as He works those changes in you?**

**Are you ready to do your part?** Read Philippians 2:12-13 (NLT) and meditate on what it means to work out your salvation (hint: part of it is to "take captive every thought to the obedience of Christ"—2 Corinthians 10:5).

## February 20: Press In

*"Who touched my clothes?" - Mark 5:30.*

Jesus is aware of your situation and hears when you seek Him. Don't be discouraged if it seems He is not responding. Keep pressing into Him and you will receive what you need, although you may be surprised at how He provides it. **Are you growing weary in seeking Him concerning your area of need?** Read the entire account in Mark 5:24-34 and then show the same determination this woman did to touch Jesus and have her need met.

## February 21: Lack

*"Why are you talking about having no bread?" - Mark 8:17.*

What you don't have can become your focus and limit what you can do and accomplish. It can also lead you into discouragement, depression and despair. If you think about what you do have, however, and ask God to bless and use it, you will be happier and more productive. **Where is your focus at present? On what you lack or what you have?** Read Judges 7 and see how the Lord used a little to accomplish His purpose and recognize that He can do the same in your own life.

## February 22: Condemnation

*"Has no one condemned you?" - John 8:10.*

When you sin, you can encounter feelings of condemnation and not fight them, concluding that you deserve to feel that way. That is wrong thinking! **Do you struggle with condemnation when you mess up? Do you feel like you deserve condemnation when you do?** Read Paul's conclusion about sin and condemnation in Romans 7:21- 8:4, and then determine to resist and refuse condemnation whenever and wherever it shows up in your life.

## February 23: How Is It?

*"What good is it for a man to gain the whole world, yet forfeit his soul?" - Mark 8:36.*

Be careful you aren't climbing a ladder that is leaning against the wrong wall! You may be making progress, but it may not be toward where you want to go. **How is it with your soul? Are you growing or stagnant? Learning or coasting? Closer to the Lord or more distant? Investing more time in career than the Lord or family?** Read Joshua's vow in Joshua 24:15, and then decide if that is a commitment you can make today with your whole heart.

## February 24: Fear of Man

*"How can you believe if you accept praise from one another, yet make no effort to obtain the praise that comes from the only God?" - John 5:44.*

You are here ultimately to please God and not be a people-pleaser. You are here specifically to please God and not please people. While there is nothing wrong with accepting praise from others, that cannot be your motivation in life, especially if it is for conduct contrary to God's will or Word. It seems in today's verse that Jesus indicated you cannot have faith in Him when your focus is on fitting in with what your culture says is praiseworthy at the expense of God's Kingdom values. **Are you compromising some aspect of your faith in order to be popular or accepted?Are you afraid of what others will say or think, thus stopping short of doing something that is in your heart to do?** Read Proverbs 29:25 and reflect on where and how the fear of man, especially those closest to you, may have crept into your walk and work.

## February 25: Sleeping

*"Why are you sleeping?" - Luke 22:46.*

It is easy to get caught up in all kinds of things and let your spiritual life wane. Or you can give so much physical energy to other things that you have none to devote to your spiritual life. When that happens, you can go to sleep spiritually and become dull to the things of God. **Are you too busy to conduct the basic devotional exercises like reading and prayer?** Read Ephesians 5:13-16 and do what you must to invest some of your time and energy in spiritual things.

## February 26: Satisfaction

*"What did you go out into the desert to see?" - Luke 7:24.*

John the Baptist had to work from a place that had enough water to baptize so the people had to travel to an inconvenient, inhospitable place to see him. People still travel to the latest, hippest place in search of an adventure or experience, yet that search is really a quest for God and the lasting peace and joy only He can provide. **What are you looking for these days? Are you restless and in pursuit of something that cannot ever satisfy your spiritual hunger? Are you seeking after spiritual experiences for the excitement or so they can equip you to do God's will?** Read John 6:35-40 and come to Jesus to have your hunger and thirst satisfied in every area of life.

## February 27: Familiarity

*"Have you never read what David did when he and his companions were hungry?" - Luke 6:3.*

Jesus wanted to teach the people, but they needed to know where He was coming from as He taught. In other words, they needed to know something about the story to which Jesus was referring in order to understand His intended lesson. The same is true for you and me. **How familiar are you with the Old Testament, and the New for that matter? What are you doing to become more familiar?** The more you know, the more God will be able to teach and impart to you. **Are you in a systematic Bible reading and/or study program?** Read Romans 15:4 to further understand why it's important that you know the Scriptures.

## February 28: Love Like God

*"If you love those who love you, what credit is that to you?" - Luke 6:32.*

God loves those who are unlovely, who don't love Him first or in return. He wants you to learn to do the same, which requires that He work His love in you first. Your love cannot depend on the worthiness or actions of others for it to be like His love. **How well do you love others who don't reciprocate, or who are not worthy of that love?** Read Romans 13:8-10 and then ask God to help you carry out what Paul described in those verses.

## February 29: Jesus

*"Who do the crowds say I am?" - Luke 9:18.*

There are always many theories and concepts of who Jesus was and is. Some say a prophet, others a holy man and still others a religious leader. Yet Jesus Himself claimed to be the Son of God, and proved it with miracles and His resurrection from the dead. **Are you influenced by the latest popular but erroneous thinking about Jesus?** Read Colossians 2:6-15 and work to develop a clear and biblical understanding of who He is in truth.

# What Would Jesus Ask You Today?

## March

## March 1: Keep Peace

*"Salt is good, but if it loses its saltiness, how can you make it salty again?" - Mark 9:50.*

Jesus went on to say that you should have salt in yourself and be at peace with others. The salt is the seasoning of God's presence that flavors what you do and say. Your salt also enables you to maintain long-term relationships with others. Take a look at Colossians 4:6 and then ask: **Am I at peace with others, or am I contentious and hard to get along with? Am I able to face times when my "salt" does lose its flavor and ask forgiveness?**

## March 2: Trials

*"Can you drink the cup I drink or be baptized with the baptism I am baptized with?" - Mark 10:38.*

Jesus was asking if the disciples were ready to suffer as He was about to suffer. **That is a good question for you as well. Are you willing to suffer for Christ's sake? Are you willing to suffer as you deny yourself, pick up your cross and follow Him?** Read 1 Peter 1:3-7 and then be ready to welcome the suffering that comes to strengthen your faith and trust in Him.

## March 3: Empower Others

*"Can a blind man lead a blind man?" - Luke 6:39.*

Many people want to help others; perhaps that is your desire. Good intentions, however, are not enough. You cannot lead others to places you have never been, and you cannot give them what you don't have. You must equip yourself if you are going to empower others. **Are you working to build yourself up so that you can build up and assist others through your expertise and experience?** Read Isaiah 50:4 and then make it your goal to build up others as God gives you opportunity.

# March 4: Give Thanks

*"Where are the other nine?" - Luke 17:17.*

Jesus healed ten lepers, but only one came back to thank Him. Jesus did a quick count and wondered where the other nine were. Being thankful requires that you are mindful of your weakness and helplessness but also aware of God's grace and mercy that sustains and energizes you. **Are you among the nine who take God's blessings for granted or the one who returns to give praise and say thanks for His love and mercy?** Read Psalm 100 and then let praise and thanksgiving be your posture throughout the day.

# March 5: Competition

*"If I want him to remain alive until I return, what is that to you?" - John 21:22.*

Peter was comparing himself to John, instead of being John's brother, and Jesus told him it was none of his business what God was working or doing in John's life. You are not in competition with others, but are called to empathize with them so you can help them or make their concerns and joys your own. **Do you take the time and make the effort to understand where others are coming from and what their needs are? Are you serving God's purpose in their lives or judging it?** Take the simple advice found in Romans 12:15 and then position yourself to support others and not compete with them.

# March 6: Understanding

*"Do you still not understand?" - Mark 8:21.*

Jesus asked this in the context of trusting Him after He had multiplied the loaves and fishes. After all He had done, the disciples still did not have faith in His ability to provide. **After all God has done for you do you have the same problem? Are you still worrying after He has been so faithful? When will you put aside your worries and**

**relax?** Read John's prayer in 3 John 2 and understand it's God's will that you prosper in all aspects of life. Then decide to walk in that provision and no longer fret over how God will provide for you.

## March 7: The Kingdom

*"What is the kingdom of God like?" - Luke 13:18.*

Jesus came proclaiming that the kingdom of God is at hand. God's Kingdom is His government, which He wants to establish in every area of your life. That includes relationships, finances, work, family and matters of thought and heart. **Are you working to bring every area of your life into alignment with God's Kingdom principles?** For some guidelines on Kingdom behavior, read Psalm 15 and then meditate on how to apply what you read.

## March 8: Self-Righteous

*"Do you think that these Galileans were worse sinners than all the other Galileans because they suffered this way?" - Luke 13:2.*

The Jews were trying to come up with a reason for a tragedy that had occurred, trying to justify themselves while seeing those victims as worse sinners than they were. Jesus told them to look to themselves, for if they did not repent, they too would perish. **Do you compare yourself to others as a means to establish your righteousness, feeling you are better than others?** You would be wise to read Luke 18:9-14 and confront your own self-righteousness wherever it exists.

## March 9: Promotion

*"Who then is the faithful and wise servant . . . ?" - Matthew 24:45.*

God does not promote nice people with good intentions. He uses those who have proven themselves faithful in the work He has put before them and those whose wisdom has grown through success and failure experiences. **Are you drawing out wisdom from your life's work to share with others? Do others consider you faithful?** Read Daniel 6:4 and you will understand why God gave Daniel a prominent position.

## March 10: Be Specific

*"What do you want me to do for you?" - Matthew 20:32.*

It is not wrong to ask God for something you need. After all, He is your heavenly Father and delights to give you good gifts as well as meet your daily needs. Yet low self-esteem, fear, or flawed thinking can prevent you from ever verbalizing what you want or need to anyone, including God. You may not believe you are worthy to receive, fearful that you are asking for the wrong thing (or too much), or think God is either not interested in or incapable of providing the mundane needs or wants you have. **Are your prayers specific? How would you answer this question if Jesus asked you right now, "What can I do for you"? Are you asking boldly or timidly, if at all?** Read Luke 11:1-13 and then ask yourself if you are being bold and forthright in prayer about your wants and needs.

## March 11: Reading

*"Have you never read . . . ?" - Matthew 21:16.*

It is said that leaders are readers. Reading expands your world and gives you creative ideas and ways of communicating and processing your own thoughts. It also gives you more substance that the Lord can quicken in you to be more useful for His purposes. **Do you read? What are you reading and why? To expand your world and learn, or simply to combat boredom?** Of course, you should read the Word as the cornerstone of any reading program, but then there should be other things that you read if you are going to grow. Read 2 Timothy 4:13 and see that Paul had a collection of books that were important to him. Do you have such a collection?

## March 12: God is Good

*"Why do you call me good?" - Mark 10:18.*

You can call God good because He is. Yet the great lie told by your enemy is that God is not good, that things which happen to you, like personal loss, death of loved ones and other tragedies, occur because God does not have your best interests in mind. **Are you struggling with God's goodness in light of current events in your life?** Read Job 1 and see how Job responded to his losses; then ask God to help you do the same.

## March 13: Thoughts

*"What do you think . . . ?" - Matthew 21:28.*

You are always thinking, in some ways talking to yourself with your thoughts. Your thoughts are where either worry or faith take root and lead to action (or inaction) on your part. **Are you aware of what you are thinking? Is your thinking helping or hindering you in your walk of faith? Are you taking steps and asking God's help to correct bad thinking?** Read Isaiah 26:3-4 and ask yourself if your thinking produces the mental peace described in this passage.

## March 14: Love Others

*"If you love those who love you,*
*what credit is that to you?" - Luke 6:32.*

There is a blessing for you if you obey the Lord and reflect His nature in your relationships. One of His traits is to love the unlovely. **Is there someone in your life with whom you are struggling? Do they treat you poorly?** Perhaps this is a time to relate to them with the love of God even though they are undeserving. Read Romans

5:6-8 to see how God loves you, and then set out today to demonstrate that same kind of love to others, especially those who are not worthy of it.

## March 15: Fasting

*"How can the guests of the bridegroom fast while he is with them?" - Mark 2:19.*

A fast is when you stop eating for a period of time to mortify your flesh and focus attention on prayer and your spiritual condition. Jesus assumed that His disciples would fast. **Do you fast at all? Why or why not?** Of course you should consult a physician before doing so, but a fast is not supposed to be easy. Read what happened in Acts 13:1-3 when the people took time to fast and minister to the Lord, and then set aside some time to do the same.

## March 16: The Only Way

*"How can Satan drive out Satan?" - Mark 3:23.*

Jesus spoke with authority regarding spiritual things because He knew what He was talking about. He was indicating that He was God, indirectly, for only God could know what Jesus taught. Jesus was not just a good moral teacher or prophet; He was and is the Son of God! **Do you believe there are other ways to God or accept that Jesus is the only one? Is that what you proclaim and teach?** Read Hebrews 1:1-4 and see that Jesus is supreme in regards to spiritual matters.

## March 17: Kingdom Behavior

*"What shall I compare the kingdom of God to?" - Luke 18:20.*

time, relationships, thoughts and attitudes, and behaviors. **Do you**

**realize that Jesus does not just want to save you, He wants to change you at the very core of your being? Do you also realize He wants to direct every area of your life, not just your church life? Have you had an encounter not only with Jesus the Savior but Jesus the King?** Read 1 Corinthians 6:8-10 to better understand what the Kingdom of God is all about. If you have time, examine where and how Jesus described the Kingdom in the gospels.

## March 18: Service at Work

*"Would he thank the servant because he did what he was told to do?" - Luke 17:9.*

You are God's servant and should not always expect to be rewarded for your obedience and faithfulness. Often your service to God is expressed to other people, and sometimes to those who don't know the Lord, especially in the area of work. **Are you serving Christ at work, or do you need to be rewarded for everything you do there, thus holding back because something is not in your job description or you are not being paid to do "that"?** Read Ephesians 6:5-8and substitute the word "employees" for "slaves" and determine how well you are serving at work, even if no reward is forthcoming. Keep in mind that God is watching and will reward you in His own way and in His perfect timing.

## March 19: Specifics

*"What do you want me to do for you?" - Mark 10:51.*

We as humans are always in need, in some kind of danger. In part, that is why we pray, and we usually cry out with requests like: "Help me!" "Save me!" "Deliver me!" There is nothing wrong with that, for if you are not specific, you are not being honest with God, hesitant to ask Him for help in all things. **Are you clear when you pray as to what you want and need God to do?** Read Psalm 3 and then be specific like David was when he cried out to the Lord.

# March 20: Peace

*"Why are you troubled, and why do doubts rise in your minds?" - Luke 24:38.*

Jesus confronted doubt and fear in the minds of His followers regularly, and nothing has changed in 2,000 years. He is still working to bring peace into your turbulent and uncertain world. You can seek this peace in external circumstances, but Jesus wants you to have peace of mind internally, regardless of what is happening around you. **Do you really believe you can have peace in the midst of life's storms?** Read Psalm 91 and rest in the truth it describes.

# March 21: Discernment

*"Why don't you judge for yourselves what is right?" - Luke 12:57.*

Jesus expects you to develop your spiritual discernment so you can assess situations and people correctly. That takes effort, knowledge of His word, and trial and error to be able to mature spiritually. Read 1 Corinthians 15:33-34 and ask yourself the question: **Am I ignorant of God and His ways? Am I growing in my ability to judge things from a spiritual perspective?** When you get your answer, set a course today that will allow you to grow and mature as you apply your faith.

# March 22: Prepared

*"For if men do these things when the tree is green, what will happen when it is dry?" - Luke 23:31.*

The real test of your spirituality can be when things are not going as you would like. Then the real "you" tends to emerge. In a sense then, you prepare in the good times for how you will respond in the bad. **What season of life are you in right now: the good or the not so good? How are you responding and are you preparing for**

**a change of season, for challenging times (dry as Jesus called them) are sure to come?** Read Philippians 4:11-13 and see how Paul prepared to live and thrive in any and all circumstances. You should prepare to do the same so you can be content in all seasons of life.

## March 23: Discussions

*"What are you discussing together as you walk along?" - Luke 24:17.*

When you get with others, you can use your words to build up or tear down, to speak idle words and gossip, or words of life, to ask questions and listen or monopolize the conversation and be insensitive to others. **How do you engage others in conversation? How can you improve?** Read Ephesians 4:29 and determine to be more gracious in your discussions.

## March 24: The Body

*"Saul, Saul, why do you persecute me?" - Acts 9:4.*

Even though Saul was persecuting believers, Jesus considered it the equivalent of persecuting Him. That is because those persecuted saints were part of His body, the body of Christ. The same is true today. How you treat God's people is an indication of how you are treating Him. Here is what John wrote in his epistle about this matter: "This is how we know what love is: Jesus Christ laid down his life for us. And we ought to lay down our lives for our brothers and sisters. **If anyone has material possessions and sees a brother or sister in need but has no pity on them, how can the love of God be in that person?** Dear children, let us not love with words or speech but with actions and in truth" (1 John 3:16-18). **How are you treating God today as you relate to His people? Are you meeting the practical needs of others in the Body? Are you moving beyond your own group and church to assist the larger worldwide Body?** What more can you do.

## March 25: Turning Back

*"You do not want to leave too, do you?" - John 6:67.*

It seems that Jesus gave His disciples every chance to turn back through hard sayings and unpopular positions that went against the grain of culture and society. He still does the same today because national, family, company, or ethnic cultures have a strong gravitational pull that seek to have their adherents comply with community standards. Yet, Jesus came to establish a new culture based on the values and standards of the kingdom of God. **Are you struggling with obedience in any area of your walk so much so that it has impacted your loyalty to the Lord or His church? Is there a culture that is seeking to keep you from identifying completely with God's kingdom culture?** Read Colossians 1:13-14 to grasp that God has transferred your citizenship to a new kingdom and then read Hebrews 11:13-16 to see that God will give people a chance to "go back" to what they left if seeking His kingdom is not to their liking.

## March 26: New Heart

*"Why do you entertain evil thoughts in your hearts?" - Matthew 9:4.*

The heart is the home for all manner of human evil. That is why God's Spirit is present in you to create a new heart. You must cooperate with His work and seek it when you are confronted with your heart problems. **How is your thought life at the moment? Are you smiling on the outside but harboring bitterness, resentment or some other evil in your heart?** Read Ezekiel 36:25-27 and then pray that this will become a reality in your life and walk with God.

## March 27: God Said

*"Have you not read what God said to you . . . ?" - Matthew 22:31.*

Notice that Jesus quoted Scripture and equated it with God speaking to you. If **Jesus had such a "high view" of Scripture, should you not have the same? Are you reading the Bible as God's word to you or just another book? If it is God's word, are you studying it to understand it more fully and completely? Do you expect to hear from Him when you read it?** Read Psalm 119:105 and then approach the Bible for what it is—God's voice to mankind.

# March 28: Memories

*"And don't you remember?" - Mark 8:18.*

When things don't go as you like, it is always good to remember all the things the Lord has done for you and times when your life was as you want it to be. **Do you have a short memory where the Lord is concerned? Do you take time to give thanks for what He has done? What can you do to enhance your memories of God's goodness in your life?** See Deuteronomy 7:17-19 and do what God commanded Israel to do: Remember what God has done!

# March 29: People

*"Do you see this woman?" - Luke 7:44.*

You encounter many people every day and may not even see them. **Do you notice the people in your world, whether they are happy or sad, joyful or burdened, weighed down or lifted up? If you don't notice the people around you, how can you effectively minister to them or receive what they have for you?** Read 1 Corinthians 11:29-32 and see that there is a price when you don't properly discern those around you who are the body of Christ.

# March 30: Clarity

*"Why is my language not clear to you?" - John 8:42.*

God is always broadcasting or speaking. You often can't hear Him because there are impediments in you that prevent you from hearing, like a hard heart, worry, preconceived notions of what He is saying or not taking time to be still and hear. **What is God saying to you today? What is He speaking to you that is for you alone? Are you spending time quietly and alone to hear what He is saying?** Read John 12:28-31 and see how people misinterpreted what God was saying, but that Jesus said the voice came and comes for you to hear!

## March 31: Memories

*"You, then, who teach others,*
*do you not teach yourself?" - Romans 2:21.*

When things don't go as you like, it is always good to remember all the things the Lord has done for you, and times when your life was as you want it to be. **Do you have a short memory where the Lord is concerned? Do you take time to give thanks for what He has done? What can you do to enhance your memories of God's goodness in your life?** Read Deuteronomy 7:17-19 and do what God commanded Israel to do: Remember what God has done!

# What Would Jesus Ask You Today?

## April

# April 1: Judging God

*"Why are you trying to trap me?" - Mark 12:15.*

God is faithful, but there are some who try to find fault with God, especially when times are tough. The devil is a willing partner in those efforts as he whispers in people's ears, "Where is God? I thought God was love? How could a loving God allow that to happen?" Then there are others who try to discover the problems and contradictions in God's word instead of reading it and then submitting to it. **Do you try to find some inconsistency with God in times when He is not meeting your expectations? Do you approach God's word to obey or to criticize?** Read Job 41 to see part of God's response to Job, or anyone for that matter, who tries to second-guess His power and love and how He employs them in human experience.

# April 2: Power

*"Am I leading a rebellion, that you have come with swords and clubs?" - Luke 22:52.*

The world only understands one kind of power and that is force—brute force in some cases. Yet the kingdom of God is based on a different power—the power of God. **Where do you put your trust? Do you put it in the legal system, money, prestige, position or in God Himself?** Read Psalm 20:6- 9 and then put your trust in God today with your whole heart.

# April 3: Power and Service

*"For who is greater, the one who is at the table or the one who serves?" - Luke 22:27.*

It's easy to say that you believe what Jesus said and then not do it. You can say, "God can do anything," but then act like God can or will do very little, especially with or through you. **Do you believe that Jesus' words are truth? Where are your actions falling short of**

**the truth you know? Where can you act on something Jesus said today concerning provision, healing, or relationships?** Read John 13:17 and then work on closing your obedience gap between Jesus' words and your behavior.

## April 4: Help

*"Do you think I cannot call on my Father, and he will at once put at my disposal more than twelve legions of angels?" - Matthew 26:53.*

Jesus had all power and authority, yet chose to submit to the Father's will by coming to earth and dying on the cross. He could have called for supernatural help, but instead put His trust in God. Sometimes suffering is an important part of God's plan for your life especially when it is suffering in the service of others. **Are you suffering now, or trying to avoid it by asking for some sort of spiritual help or relief?** Read Colossians 1:24 and see that Paul suffered on behalf of others for the cause of Christ. You should be ready to do the same.

## April 5: Forsaken

*"My God, my God, why have you forsaken me?" - Matthew 27:46.*

Jesus asked this question on the cross and, at first glance, it appears to be a question of despair. Yet the question is the opening line to Psalm 22, which starts out in questioning despair but ends in hope and triumph. **Are you in the midst of a life crisis that feels like God has abandoned you? Do you know someone who is?** If so, look at Psalm 22 and take or give encouragement based on the truth found in the psalm.

## April 6: Fulfilled

*"But how then would the Scriptures be fulfilled that say it*

*must happen in this way?" - Matthew 26:54.*

What happened during Easter week was planned by God for the salvation of the world. Jesus was a willing participant in this plan and not a victim. His commitment was to the Word of God to ensure all that must happen did. **If Jesus was that committed to see the Word of God fulfilled, can you be any less? Where can you submit to God's plan, regardless of cost?** Look at Paul's commitment to God's will in Philippians 1:18-24 and determine to do the same by God's grace.

## April 7: Assumptions

*"Woman, why are you crying?*
*Who is it you are looking for?" - John 20:15.*

Jesus asked Mary this question at the empty tomb, but she did not recognize him because she thought He was dead. She knew Jesus and certainly should have recognized His voice, but she was not expecting to see or hear Him so she did neither. Your wrong assumptions can cause you to miss the obvious, something that is right in front of you, which others can see but you cannot. **Where has your thinking limited your faith effectiveness? Are you ready to ask God to show you any of your blind spots that are holding you back? What assumptions do you carry that hinder your ability to grow and learn?** Read the story of Hagar in Genesis 21:8-21 and see how her assumption blinded her to an oasis right before her eyes. Then see if your assumptions and thinking are doing the same.

## April 8: Impediments

*"Why is my language not clear to you?" - John 8:43.*

God is a superb communicator, so if something is not clear to you, there is some impediment in your mind preventing you from understanding what He is saying. It can be an attitude, assumption, worry, fear, doubt, or hardness of heart. **Are you prepared to ask the Lord**

**to show you what it is? Are you ready to deal with it when He reveals it to you?** Read Luke 24:13-32 and see how two disciples could not recognize Jesus or understand His suffering since they thought He was dead, even though they were well acquainted with and loved Him. Then see if you are like those disciples in any area of your life.

## April 9: Grow

*"How then will you believe if I speak of heavenly things?" - John 3:12.*

Jesus desires that you grow in your understanding of the things of God. Notice, however, this learning requires faith, for you must believe God is leading you into this understanding. **Where does this understanding come from?** It comes from both experience and being firmly grounded in God's word. Let your prayer be the one found in Psalm 119:18, then have faith God will answer your prayer!

## April 10: Details

*"When I broke the five loaves for the five thousand, how many basketfuls of pieces did you pick up?" - Mark 8:19.*

It is interesting that Jesus asked the disciples how many baskets were left over after He multiplied the loaves. There was a lesson in the details, for Jesus did not provide just enough, He provided more than enough. **Do you remember the details of what God has done for you in the past? Do you use those details to encourage you today?** Read 1 Kings 19:10-18 and see how God used details to lift the spirit of a downcast prophet and allow Him to do the same for you today.

## April 11: Conversations

*"You of little faith, why are you talking among*

*yourselves about having no bread?" - Matthew 16:8.*

You have the power to encourage and motivate others to be all they can be. When you talk with friends or family, you can use the time to build them up, be neutral and do nothing constructive, or tear them down and discourage them. **What is your purpose when you meet with others? What do you discuss when you get with your friends or family? Do you talk about the good things or the not so good? Do you ask them questions about their lives or monopolize conversations to talk about you? Are you pessimistic or optimistic?** Read Proverbs 18:21 to understand the power in your words and Malachi 3:16 to understand that the Lord is listening when you have your conversations with others.

## April 12: Traditions

*"Why are you angry with me for healing the whole man on the Sabbath?" - John 7:23.*

The Jews were angry because Jesus violated a tradition they thought was from God's law. **Do you have traditions that cause you to ignore God's law? Do you not give even though you know it's God's will to be generous? Do you avoid assembling with God's people even though you know God requires it?** Read Mark 7:1-23 and ask God to show you if you are guilty of doing what Jesus described.

## April 13: The Lost

*"Will he not leave the ninety-nine on the hills and go to look for the one that wandered off?" - Matthew 18:13.*

Jesus is a good shepherd who seeks those who are lost, and He expects us to do the same. **What are you doing these days to reach the lost? Are you at least praying for those who may have wandered off from the faith? How often do you share your own faith? Are you supporting those who are pursuing the lost through**

**missions and evangelism?** Read what some did in Acts 11:19-21, and then see how you can go and do the same.

## April 14: More Valuable

*"Are you not much more valuable than they?"*
*- Matthew 6:27.*

God has promised to provide for you, no matter the circumstances. Yet you can panic when things don't come according to your timetable. Then you need to remind yourself that you are more valuable than the rest of creation, which God provides for abundantly and regularly. **If that's the case, then why would you think He would not provide for you and your family? Are you uptight and anxious over how and when God is going to provide for your needs? Do you thank God for what you have today and what He will provide tomorrow? Do you confuse your needs with your wants, forgetting that if you don't have "it" right now you may not need it right now?** Read Psalm 111 and learn to relax in the certainty of God's promise of provision.

## April 15: Radical Obedience

*"If I am telling the truth, why don't you believe me?"*
*- John 8:46.*

Jesus expressed His ministry as an itinerate teacher who eventually had a group of people following Him to monitor HIs every word and find fault. He addressed many issues and often Jesus had to assure His listeners He was telling the truth because their spiritual condition was so subnormal that when He said something normal, they thought it was abnormal! **What about you? Do you consider what Jesus said about giving, forgiveness, obedience, or some other issue an ideal and not a command to carry out? Are you ready to obey what Jesus said even if it seems out of the realm of possibility for you to achieve?** Read two of these examples in Matthew 17:20-21 and Matthew 18:21-22 and then determine to live a life of radical obedience to an abnormal message.

## April 16: Bold Prayer

*"Which of you, if his son asks for bread, will give him a stone?" - Matthew 7:9.*

The context for this question is that God is your Father and He will give good things to those who ask Him. **How dynamic is your prayer life? For what are you asking and believing the Lord? Are you hesitant to ask or bold to make your requests known to God?** Read Psalm 145:19 and then make sure your prayer life is active, exciting and full of life.

## April 17: Specific Prayer

*"What do you want me to do for you?" - Luke 18:41.*

Jesus asked this of a blind man, and the answer would seem obvious, yet Jesus asked him anyway. Perhaps He wanted to see if the man really wanted healed or had instead become comfortable with his problem. **What would your answer be if He asks you that question today? Are you clear or ambivalent? Bold or apologetic? Specific or general? Addressing personal needs or those of someone else?** Read Hebrews 5:7-10 and then emulate Jesus' fervor and intensity when He prayed as you ask God for specific things.

## April 18: Futility

*"Since you cannot do this very little thing, why do you worry about the rest?" - Luke 12:26.*

That's an important question: Why do you worry? For some, worry is a superstitious act, believing it is something they can do to ensure that their desired outcome is produced. They believe their pessimism can keep them from being disappointed and help produce something good. For others, it is an attempt to stay in control of their world, giving them something they can do while they wait on the Lord. **What possible good can worry accomplish? How much energy have you lost to this futile, mental effort, yet you continue to engage in it? Do you see worry as the sin that it is or just as a bad habit?** Read and pray Psalm 26 and then work to make the truth in that psalm a reality in your own life and walk with the Lord.

## April 19: Questions

*"Why question me?" - John 18:21.*

You seek the Lord and ask Him questions so you can gain insight and understanding. Someone once said that quality questions lead to a quality life, but only if you get quality answers—and where can you get better answers than from the Lord! **Are you seeking the Lord? What questions are you asking Him? Are you willing to ask until He answers?** Read Proverbs 2:2-5 and notice the intensity with which you must seek if you expect to hear.

## April 20: Finish Well

*"What good will it be for a man if he gains the whole world, yet forfeits his soul?" - Matthew 16:25.*

The answer to this question is "No good," but that does not stop people from seeking to fill their spiritual void with things. **Where is your main priority? Do you invest as much or more in your spiritual growth than your physical life? Do you give God His time on Sunday and take the rest, or do you devote daily energy to feed and strengthen your spiritual being?** Read how Solomon gained the whole world but forfeited his soul in 1 Kings 11:1-6, and determine to finish well by seeking God all the days of your life.

## April 21: Rich or Poor

*"Or why do you look down on your brother?"*
*- Romans 14:10.*

You are no better than anyone else in God's family, even those who mess up badly or how much good you have done. As the old saying goes, there for the grace of God goes any one of us! That also pertains to how much you own or don't own for your wealth and possessions (or lack thereof) do not speak to your spirituality or standing with God. **Are you judging someone who has done wrong, maybe even wronged you? Do you fail to see your own spiritual poverty as you look down on someone else? Have you fallen for the thinking that trusting God is a way to wealth which indicates a special standing before Him?** Read Proverbs 18:23 and then determine into which category you belong, the poor or the rich. Then read the parable in Luke 12:13-21 to be reminded that trusting in riches is quite foolish.

## April 22: His Grace

*"What do you have that you did not receive?"*
*- 1 Corinthians 4:7.*

You did not earn any of your spiritual gifts, insight, or standing in the Lord, even if you have worked hard, studied, and applied yourself to the things of God. It was all His gift of grace to you, so therefore there is no room for pride or arrogance where His work in your life is concerned. **Are you feeling a bit smug about your abilities or insight? Do you have little patience for those who cannot match your performance due to your years in the Lord or your experience in walking with Him? Are you freely giving away what you have freely received?** Read 2 Samuel 11 and see that for all his history in the Lord, David was not above pride that led to failure and you aren't either—so walk humbly.

## April 23: Body Treatments

*"Saul! Saul! Why do you persecute me?" - Acts 22:7.*

Saul was persecuting followers of Jesus, but Jesus saw it as if Saul was persecuting Him personally. That tells us that what we do to, with, and for God's people we are really doing to God, for good or not so good. **How are you treating God's people these days? Are you gracious and forgiving, or cold and detached? Are you building meaningful relationships with them so you can know their needs and help where possible? What more can you do?** One thing is to read 1 Thessalonians 5:12-15 and evaluate your behavior in each area that Paul mentioned therein.

## April 24: Old Testament

*"Haven't you read what David did when he and his companions were hungry?" - Matthew 12:3.*

The story Jesus referred to is found in the Old Testament in 1 Samuel 21. When you think of it, Jesus only had the Old Testament to preach and teach from, and He did a powerful job of communicating God's truth. **How familiar are you with the Old Testament? Is it part of your regular reading program? Are you familiar with its stories and can you refer to them as a teaching aide?** Read 2 Peter 1:19-21 and then find and follow a reading program that will help you become more familiar and comfortable with the Old Testament.

## April 25: Commotion

*"Why all this commotion and wailing?" - Mark 5:39.*

It is easy to become upset when you think something is wrong, only to find out you did not have all the information or you jumped to the wrong conclusion. If you are not careful, this can become a bad habit, and you find yourself wasting a lot of emotional energy. **Are you regularly upset; your mind occupied with negative thoughts?** Read this short verse in 1 Peter 5:6-7 and see that it is a command! Then work to eliminate the commotion in your mind caused by bad thinking.

## April 26: Soothing Tongue

*"How can you who are evil say anything good?" - Matthew 12:34.*

The Bible has a lot to say about words and things you say because what you say has power for good or not-so-good. The problem, however, is not just what you say, but what you don't say when you miss an opportunity to lift someone up. **Are you not saying encouraging or positive things you should to those closest to you?** Read Proverbs 15:4 and set your mind, with God's help, to be that "soothing tongue" that brings healing through what you say.

## April 27: Headquarters

*"John's baptism—where did it come from? Was it from heaven, or from men?" - Matthew 21:25.*

In this question, Jesus acknowledged that there are some spiritual things invented by man, but some that come from God. It is critical that you know the difference and respond accordingly. **What is heaven doing in your life right now? What is the Lord 'saying' through circumstances or His word that is a message to you from your spiritual headquarters?** Read Psalm 29, then see where 'heaven' is speaking to you and respond accordingly.

## April 28: Invest the Time

*"Do you still not understand?" - Matthew 16:9.*

Jesus spent considerable time and effort in teaching and training His disciples, and He at times rebuked them for being dull and slow. If those disciples needed that much input and correction, then we can expect the same amount if we want to be effective and useful in God's service. God wants you to grow in your understanding of who He is and what He requires of you. If you don't invest time and effort into your growth, however, you will not develop and mature—and that is a dangerous thing. And even when you invest the time, you will have to still have to review and relearn to keep things fresh and relevant. **What is your plan for spiritual growth? What are you reading? What are you studying? What classes are you taking? Are you helping others 'understand'?** Read Hosea 4:4-9 and see the danger in not paying the price to learn and grow spiritually.

## April 29: Healing

*"Which is easier: to say, 'Your sins are forgiven,' or to say, 'Get up and walk'?" - Matthew 9:5.*

Jesus' opponents were watching Him to see if He would heal and then He threw them a curve when He also forgave a man's sins. Their response was, "Who can forgive sins except God alone?" which was the point Jesus was trying to make: He was and is God. He was also showing that nothing is too difficult for the Lord. If you can have faith that God has forgiven your sins, then you can also believe He can preserve your health or heal your body. Both are miracles of which you are not worthy, but both are gracious acts that He delights to perform for His people. **Are you in need of healing? Do you believe He can? Do you believe He wants to?** Read Exodus 15:26 and then trust the Lord your Healer to do what He promised He would do!

## April 30: Good Old Days

*"How is it that you don't know how to interpret this present time?" - Luke 12:56.*

Every generation can resist the new generation and its music, customs and dress, yearning for the good old days of the past. That leads to intolerance and, where church is concerned, a gap that hinders evangelism and community. **How do you feel about the generation behind you? Ahead of you? Can you accept this generation's culture and still focus on love and service?** Read 1 John 2:12-14 where John had something to say for all generations; that is how you should be too.

# What Would Jesus Ask You Today?

## May

## May 1: Authority

*"Do you want to be free from fear of the one in authority?" - Romans 13:3.*

Jesus did not ask this question, but He modeled the answer He was free from fear of authority, whether Roman or Jewish, because He always did the right things. Therefore He had nothing to hide or cover up. **How do you relate to those in authority? Do you see them as put in place by the Lord? Do you have things to hide or can you be open and honest? How do speak concerning those in authority? Do you honor the office God instituted or do you speak badly of those He has assigned to leadership positions?** Read Proverbs 28:1 and see into which category you fit where authority is concerned.

## May 2: Looking Down

*"Or why do you look down on your brother" - Romans 14:10.*

When you look down at people, it's because you believe you are "above" them in some way. And that is never a good posture to be in, for you can "fall down" at any time, especially if God sets a trap to catch you in your pride. **Do you see yourself as superior or better than some people? Are they in the church? Does it lead you to avoid them or talk about them when absent?** Read James 2:1-13 and search your heart to see if you have indeed looked down on others.

## May 3: Obedience Gap

*"If I am telling the truth, why don't you believe me?" - John 8:47.*

It's easy to say that you believe what Jesus said and then not do it. You can say, "God can do anything," but then act like God can or will do very little. **Do you believe that Jesus' words are truth? Where are your actions falling short of the truth you know? Where can you act on something Jesus said today concerning provision, healing or relationships?** Read John 13:17 and then work on closing your obedience gap between Jesus' words and your behavior.

## May 4: Outsiders

*"And if you greet only your brothers, what are you doing more than others?" - Matthew 5:47.*

If you are only nice and gracious to other believers, your circle of influence for the Lord will not expand. Your commitment to the Lord and the evidence of His work in your life will shine when you are mistreated and you respond with kindness and grace. **Is there someone in life who is less than friendly to you? For the Lord's sake, can you treat this person as Jesus would?** Read Luke 6:29-36 and determine to do what Jesus taught concerning those outside the family of God.

## May 5: Fretting

*"Who of you by worrying can add a single hour to his life?" - Matthew 6:27.*

Jesus confronted the issues of worry and fear regularly in His earthly ministry, probably because they are such common and prevalent enemies of your faith. This question puts it all into perspective, for in essence worry is a futile exercise and waste of energy! What's more, it is sinful behavior. **Are you fretting over the future and all the things that can go wrong? Do you worry about circumstances beyond your control but worry it anyway? Did a family member teach you to worry?** If so, then you can learn to un-worry. Read Psalm 37:7-9, which uses the word fret instead of worry, and then be careful to follow its commands if you are serious about overcoming worry and replacing it with confident trust in the God of your future.

# May 6: Answers

*"Who do people say the Son of Man is?"*
*- Matthew 16:13.*

Secular culture often tries to define who Jesus is, with new books appearing that contain fantastic theories that usually try to explain away Jesus' divinity or tarnish Jesus' humanity. Yet Jesus did not ask His enemies or the casual onlookers who He was; He asked His closest disciples. And we learn from the gospel accounts that there was a wide variety of theories among the populace ranging from Him being John the Baptist resurrected to one of the prophets of old. Jesus then pressed them and Peter gave his well-known answer, "You are the Messiah, the Son of the living God" (Matthew 16:16). Jesus is still asking His disciples today: **"Who am I?" What is your answer? Do you have a ready response to those who may ask you? Is it clear and biblical accurate?** Read John 1:1-18 and see if you can get any answers in John's introduction as to who Jesus is so you can respond when asked—by the Lord or others.

# May 7: Honesty

*"Why are you thinking these things?" - Mark 2:8.*

Some find it inappropriate to say certain things to the Lord, even though they are thinking them. Jesus knows your thoughts before you speak them. Therefore, you can speak your heart and be honest without fear. This can transform your prayer life from reciting a list of needs to pouring out your heart to Him. **How honest are with the Lord?** Read Psalm 139:1-6 and determine to be more open and honest in your times of prayer and communication with God.

# May 8: Faith Actions

*"You foolish man, do you want evidence that faith without deeds is useless?" - James 2:20.*

Your faith must lead to some type of action or it is worthless. And there is always something you can do in faith, like writing a letter, speaking the right words or making a visit to someone. **Where has your faith become "useless"? What can you do to activate your faith through appropriate actions? Where is fear keeping you from acting?** Read 2 Kings 4:18-37 and see how the faith actions of the woman in that story saved her son's life. Then go and imitate her faith.

## May 9: Women Gifts

*"Why are you bothering her?" - Mark 14:6.*

The disciples were harassing a woman who had bestowed an extravagant gift on Jesus, and He ordered them to stop bothering her. That is good advice for the church, which needs to honor the gifts God has given to the women in its midst. **If you are a woman, do you work to showcase who God made you to be regardless of how men react? If you are a man, do you accept women as partners in life and work?** Read Acts 16:11-15 and see how God worked in and through Lydia and make sure you are allowing the same to happen with other Lydia's in your midst.

## May 10: Good Company

*"For which of these do you stone me?" - John 10:32.*

Jesus was certainly persecuted for righteousness sake, and you will be too as you carry out your purpose work that He has assigned for you to do. So if you are suffering, it is probably not because you have done something wrong but something right! **Are you suffering for His sake? Are there those who oppose your work and slander or criticize you?** Then you are in good company! Read Romans 5:1-5 and see Paul's response to suffering that was a result of his God-given work.

# May 11: The Gospels

*"Are you asking one another what I meant when I said . . . ?" - John 16:19.*

Disciples of any leader usually study that leader's sayings and philosophy. As a follower of Christ you should study His sayings as well. Of course those are found in the four gospels, each with its own target audience and purpose for being written. **What is your favorite gospel? How often do you read it and the others? Is your familiarity and understanding of Jesus' sayings growing?** Read Luke 6:46-49 to see what Jesus said about those who do and do not heed His sayings.

# May 12: Focus

*"How many loaves do you have?" - Mark 6:38.*

Your tendency may be to focus on what you don't have, but this question asks you to inventory what you do have. Once you see that, you can then focus on how the Lord can take what you have and supplement it with His miraculous provision, for nothing is too difficult for Him. **Where is your focus? On what you have or on what you don't have? Do you see that God can use your little and do much, but only if you release it to Him? Are you trusting God to expand what you have so you can do even more?** Read the story of Elijah and the widow in 1 Kings 17:7-16 and see what lessons you can apply from that to your own situation.

# May 13: Fear of Death

*"Whoever lives and believes in me will never die. Do you believe this?" - John 11:26.*

Jesus came to destroy the power that the fear of death had over human life by granting eternal life to anyone who put their trust in Him. The result has been that those who knew Him could face death in persecution because they knew there was a life to come. If death is the worst that can happen to you, and the fear of that has been taken away, then you should be a fearless person, knowing that your life can never end. **Are you afraid? Of what? What has you bound so that you cannot flow freely in doing God's will?** Read 1 Corinthians 15:20-26 and then examine where in your life fear has taken away your ability to function as God would have you to do.

## May 14: Study

*"David calls him 'Lord.' How then can he be his son?" - Luke 20:44.*

Jesus was quizzing the Jews about a passage of Scripture that was difficult to understand. It was not difficult for Him, however, and He regularly explained those passages to His disciples. **Are you reading and seeking to find those insights for yourself? By what means? Reading? Classes? A college degree? Discussion groups?** Read 2 Timothy 2:15 and work to accomplish what the verse commands you to do and be.

## May 15: Let Them Go

*"How do you know, wife, whether you will save your husband? Or, how do you know, husband, whether you will save your wife?" - 1 Corinthians 7:16.*

The answer to today's questions is that you don't know. The point is that you cannot change anyone else, even those closest to you; only God can do that. You can influence them, but they still have to make up their own mind about serving the Lord and following His will for their lives. **Are you trying to do more in someone's life than you are capable of doing? Do you want to see them change more than they do?** Then perhaps it's time to 'let them go' and release them to the Lord's care. Read John 21:20-22 and then heed Jesus' response to Peter's question about John.

# May 16: Hardening

*"Are your hearts hardened?" - Mark 8:17.*

A heart affects what you hear, see, say, and do for the Lord. It is a gradual process for the hardening to occur, but the hardening stems from decisions when you choose to ignore God's voice through His word, through others, or as He speaks to your heart. The only way to determine if your heart is hard is to ask the Lord to show you and then to pay attention for His answer, realizing that your hardening makes it harder to hear Him. **Are you suffering from 'hardening of the heart-eries'? Are you as zealous for the things of the Lord as you once were? Do you settle now for church attendance instead of private prayer and study? Do you seek the Lord and wait for His answers like you once did?** Heed the warning in Hebrews 3:15 and go about the business of maintaining a soft heart where the Lord and His purposes for you are concerned.

# May 17: Thinking

*"What do you think, Simon?" - Matthew 17:25.*

Take out Simon's name and put your name in the question above. Do you know what you think? God does not want you to check your brain at the door of the church; He wants you to renew your mind so that your thinking is correct and godly. **If the goal of the Spirit in you is to give you the mind of Christ, when do you think you get that mind? After 20 years in the Lord? Or 30? Or could you have it today?** Read Luke 1:1-4 and notice how natural it was for Luke to conclude that he was to write his gospel. That is how it should be with you.

# May 18: Effort

*"But what did you go out to see?" - Luke 7:26.*

The people of Jesus' generation made great effort to go see John the

Baptist in the desert because they were looking for the Messiah. They paid a price to follow and pursue what they valued. **What do you pay a price to see? The things of God or the latest cultural fad? Do you make greater effort to pursue your hobby or a movie than you do spiritual matters?** Read Exodus 23:7 to see the price that the men of Israel had to pay to be in God's presence and then determine not to do any less in your day and generation.

## May 19: Simplicity

*"Why do you stand here looking into the sky?" - Acts 1:11.*

While heaven should be of interest to any believer, the truth is that you will get there soon enough. Right now, your focus is to be on earthly things as you represent God wherever He has placed you. You are also not to be infatuated with when He will return or end times speculation, for that too will happen in due time in a way that is according to God's purpose. **Where is your focus? Are you gazing into things that don't really matter, or are you looking to maximize your time here by fulfilling your purpose? Is your time spent on end time theories and speculation or on building God's kingdom in the here and now?** Read 1 Thessalonians 4:1-12 and follow the simple life philosophy spelled out in those verses.

## May 20: God's Enemies

*"Why are you trying to kill me?" - John 7:19.*

It is hard to imagine that there were people who hated Jesus and actually plotted not just to undermine Him but also to kill Him. The Church today is persecuted in many places around the globe because the persecutors hate Him as well, just like the Jewish leaders did. **Are you encountering persecution that is not due to your own failures and for which there may be no explanation? Do you see that persecution is a supernatural response to your decision to follow Christ? Have you considered that you are only being persecuted because of your love for God and His Son Jesus?** Read Matthew

5:10-12 and then keep in mind that you are blessed if and when you are persecuted by God's enemies for representing Him here on earth. Peter went farther and outlined the attitude and behavior you should have if you are indeed suffering for the cause of Christ in1 Peter 2:19-25. If you are not being persecuted, then pray for those in other parts of the world who are.

## May 21: Good

*"Why do you ask me about what is good?" - Matthew 19:7.*

You must not rely on other sources, like political parties, the media, family, denominational traditions, or your best friend to tell you what is right and good. And where does God most often reveal what is good? In His word, of course. **Are you allowing God to define the good in your life? Do you evaluate your activities based on His word or on another source?** Read Matthew 15:1-11 and ask God to show where you have allowed tradition to trump God's good in your life.

## May 22: Humanity

*"Do you have anything here to eat?" - Luke 24:41.*

Jesus asked the disciples this question after He rose from the dead. Why? Perhaps the reason was to show that He was still human in every way, except for sin. This is important because One like us is now seated at the right hand of the Father and can still empathize with us concerning our human condition. **Do you need someone who understands your situation and can help?** If so, then read Hebrews 2:14-18 and learn to draw on the strength only Jesus can give, not just as God, but also as your elder brother.

## May 23: Weak & Miserable

*"How is it that you are turning back to those weak and miserable principles?" - Galatians 4:9.*

When you are set free in Christ, it is ridiculous to resort back to empty practices like horoscopes, superstitions and good luck charms. It is also futile to pursue strategies that exalt the wisdom of man as opposed to the wisdom of God! **Where are you still in bondage or resorting to weak and miserable principles that have not helped you to this point? When will you turn to completely do things God's way?** Read Acts 9:8-24 about a man named Simon who had turned to God but acted in accordance with weak and miserable principles.

## May 24: Enslaved

*"How is it that you are turning back to those weak and miserable principles?" - Galatians 4:9.*

You you are set free in Christ, it makes no sense to turn back to useless practices like horoscopes, superstitions, good luck charms, playing the lottery, or resorting to other get-rich-quick schemes. It is also futile to pursue strategies that exalt the wisdom of man as opposed to the wisdom of God. **Where are you still in bondage or resorting to weak and miserable principles and practices that have not helped you to this point in your life? When will you totally commit to do things God's way?** Read Acts 9:8-24 to learn about a man named Simon who had turned to God but continued to act in accordance with weak and miserable principles, and it almost cost him dearly.

## May 25: More Beautiful

*"What do you have that you did not receive?" - 1 Corinthians 4:7.*

Your gifts, opportunities, looks, personality, insight and strengths all came from the Lord, so you cannot be proud about what you have. Yet you can be honest about what you have and determine to use it for God's glory without being proud, and then work to maximize them all. **What did you receive from the Lord? How can you make**

**it more effective and productive for Him?** Read Esther 2:7-9 and see that Esther's beauty was God's doing, but how she was given treatments to be even more beautiful. Then determine to do the same thing with what God has given you to be or do for Him.

# May 26: Clarity

*"Do you understand what you are reading?" - Acts 8:30.*

Phillip heard the Ethiopian reading in his chariot as he departed Jerusalem for his home. Today's question assumes that you, like the Ethiopian, are reading the Bible and perhaps other related material. It also presumes you are not just reading, but reading to comprehend and apply what you learn to your life. The eunuch needed someone to help him understand what he was reading and so do you. **Do you have a Bible reading program? Do you have a strategy to get your questions answered about the Word? Do you have a reading program to supplement the Word? Who regularly gives you insight into the Word to help you grasp the meaning and process an application?** Read Nehemiah 8:1-8 and see that the people listened to the Word but also had someone helping them clarify the meaning. You should approach the Word in the same manner.

# May 27: Harvest

*"Do you not say, 'Four months more and then the harvest?'" - John 4:35.*

Jesus went on to say after this question, "Open your eyes and look at the fields! They are ripe for harvest." Of course, He was talking about lives to be won for His kingdom. As He said this, they were standing in Samaria when Jesus had just had His encounter with the woman at the well. **Are you stuck in a bias against some group of people who God loves and wants to reach, like the disciples in regards to the Samaritans? Do you see ripe fields, or are you focused on how bad things are in the world? Are you shaking your head at rampant sin, or do you see that as an indication that many**

**people who are hungry and searching for God?** Read1 Peter 3:15-16 and then do your part to lead people to Christ by being ready to provide the answers they seek where Christ is concerned.

## May 28: Repent

*"How long shall I put up with you?" - Mark 9:19.*

The good news is that God 'puts up' with us a long time, but even God's patience has limits. Yet even when God works to discipline you, it is for your own good and the judgment is seldom as severe as it could be. Don't take advantage of God's grace, however, and mistake it for acceptance of your behavior or attitude. but rather endeavor to change with His help. **Are you testing the limits of God's patience?** Read Romans 2:4 and then ask God to show you where you need to repent, which merely means turning around and moving in the opposite direction.

## May 29: Redemption

*"Whose portrait is this? And whose inscription?" - Mark 12:16.*

The Jews tried to trap Jesus by either condemning the Roman government or siding with it against His own people, but He turned the tables by giving His well-known, "give unto Caesar" response. Jesus did not condemn politics per se, but rather instructed the listeners to be righteous in their dealings with others, regardless of their chosen work or profession. **Do you see the world's institutions as evil and places to be avoided, or do you consider them all to be part of God's creation in need of redemption and His kingdom rule?** This will determine whether you get involved in the world outside the church or choose to sit on the sideline to criticize and condemn. Read Colossians 1:19-20 and see that God's will is to reconcile and redeem all things to Christ, which includes education, business, the arts, and even politics.

# May 30: Pagans

*"Do not even pagans do that?" - Matthew 5:47.*

The world is consistently disappointed when they look to see something different in the church and can't find it. What are they looking for? Usually they expect to see love and care for the needy and downtrodden. When that is absent, they dismiss the church as irrelevant. **Is your behavior distinct from the pagans among whom you live? When pagans see you, do they acknowledge that you live by your convictions and represent Christ?** Read 1 Peter 3:8-17 and then be prepared to live a lifestyle that glorifies God and His work in your life.

# May 31: Can't See

*"How is it you don't understand that I was not talking to you about bread?" - Matthew 16:11.*

It is possible for you not to understand God and His Word because of assumptions, preconceived notions, bad thinking or bad teaching you have heard. The Bible is truth, but your perception of truth can be flawed. The problem is greater when your assumption is that you know when you really don't. **How can you know when this is happening in your life?** Read Philippians 3:3-6 to see Saul's spiritual pedigree and realize that he could not see the truth until Jesus opened his eyes. Ask Jesus to show you any area in your life where you have the same problem.

# What Would Jesus Ask You Today?

## June

## June 1: Ask Questions

*"While Jesus was teaching in the temple courts, he asked, 'How is it . . . ?'" - Mark 12:35.*

Jesus asked a lot of questions when He taught, trying to draw people out and help them think. **If you are teaching, do you ask a lot of questions? If you are working one-on-one with others, do you talk more than you listen?** If so, asking good questions can help you be a better listener and more effective in helping and teaching others. Read James 1:19-20 and use asking questions as a means to accomplish what these verses tell you to do.

## June 2: Both

*"Which is easier: to say, 'Your sins are forgiven,' or to say, 'Get up and walk'" - Luke 5:23.*

Of course Jesus was and is able to perform both actions; He can forgive sins and heal. But His contemporaries were not convinced He could do either! **How about you? Do you go to Jesus for forgiveness? Do you also go for healing? Have you forgiven yourself if He has indeed forgiven you? And even if you seek medical help, do you see Jesus as your ultimate source of healing?** Read Matthew 8:16-17 and realize that Jesus came to heal all the infirmities of your body and the soul.

## June 3: God's Patience

*"O unbelieving generation, how long shall I stay with you?" - Mark 9:19.*

Jesus had just come down from the Mount of Transfiguration when he confronted angry leaders, ineffective followers, a desperate father, and an epileptic son. He expressed His exasperation before He silenced the first, rebuked and taught the second, counseled with the third, and healed the fourth. God is patient, but you must never mistake HIs patience for acceptance of your attitudes, beliefs, or behaviors that are contrary to His will. His kindness simply provides you time to repent and turn in the direction of God's' will. **Is there something in your life that you know is unacceptable, yet you tolerate it, counting on God's silence so you can continue? Are you at a place where you should be a leader but still cannot bear fruit in your walk with Him?** Then you may want to reconsider as you read Hebrews 5:11-14 and 2 Peter 3:9 to see that God is giving you plenty of room to act before He does!

## June 4: Where's God?

*"While people say to me all day long, 'Where is your God?'" - Psalm 42:3.*

There are always some who watch to see how you will respond to adversity, and they may be quick to raise a question about God's faithfulness. They don't understand how God uses adversity to shape and mold you, or that eventually the trial will end and a blessing will come. **Are you going through a tough time? Are people questioning God's faithfulness toward you? Are you?** Encourage yourself with Psalm 30:5 and then watch for the morning of God's joy to break forth at just the right time, maybe even today.

## June 5: Clarity

*"Then Jesus asked him, 'What is your name?'" - Mark 5:9.*

When confronted with evil, Jesus asked the demon what his name was. When dealing with a spiritual problem in your own life, you need the same kind of clarity. **What is its name? Is it unforgiveness, anger, bitterness, fear, or rejection?** That requires that you ask and keep on asking until you get the answer you need, and then taking the necessary steps to be set free. Read Psalm 51 and then strive to have the same kind of honesty and clarity that David had when he was facing a sin problem in his own life.

# June 6: Get Noticed

*"Instead, don't you put it on its stand?" - Mark 4:21.*

Jesus was asking this in reference to a light, but He wasn't concerned about lamps. He was referring to you allowing your light to shine so that all may see what God is doing in your life. He was also urging His listeners to do good deeds to be noticed so that God may be glorified. **Are you practicing a false humility that keeps you from "showing off' what God has done in your life? Are you appropriately showcasing His gifts and fruit?** Read Ephesians 2:10, and then accept the fact that some of the good deeds God has for you to do will be noticed and discussed by others. So be it!

# June 7: Growing

*"How then will you understand any parable?" - Mark 4:13.*

The disciples understood Jesus' parables only after they had asked Him for the meaning. That is how you will understand the parables or anything else in God's Word for that matter. You must pay attention and not assume you know what a passage or verse means, but seek Him for the meaning and keep looking to extract any and all of what God issaying. **Are you growing in your understanding of God's Word?** It's long, but read part, or all, of Psalm 119 that beautifully describes the power and role of God's word in your life.

# June 8: Lay Them Down

*"Or what can a man give in exchange for his soul" - Mark 8:37.*

Jesus was clear: If you want to save your life you must lose it. That means you must trust the Lord for the fullness of life and joy you crave and not try to find it by selfish means. **Where are you striving for self-fulfillment or purpose in your own strength? Where do you need to lay down your interests as you understand them**

**and pursue God's interests, which are ultimately your own best interests?** Read Psalm 49:7-9 and see there is no price you can pay for salvation and joy except to yield your life totally and completely to God and His purpose for you.

## June 9: Confess

*"Simon son of John, do you truly love me?" - John 21:16.*

Jesus had a one-on-one with Peter to help him face up to and move on from his denial of the Lord. From this question, you see that Jesus knows your name, your family background and with which spiritual issues you are struggling. There is no need for you to hide, but you can run to Him with your sins and problems instead of running away. **Are you being less than forthright in your communion with God these days? What are you afraid of or trying to hide?** Read 1 John 1:8-10 and then confess your sins with the confidence that He already knows and is ready to forgive.

## June 10: Following Him

*"Jesus saw them following and asked, 'What do you want?'" - John 1:38.*

Some men were following Jesus and wanted to know where He lived. Jesus turned and asked them what they wanted, for He knew they were looking for more than information; they were looking for their purpose. **If you are following Jesus, what do you want? What are you looking for?** You may be curious, you may have needs to be met, or perhaps you want to know more about God. **Do you want to know God and His will for you as you follow?** That is the most important reason of all. Read Deuteronomy 6:4-9 and see that your following Him is not to be a casual but an all-consuming process in which you will learn to love Him with all your heart, soul, mind, and strength.

# June 11: A Sign

*"He sighed deeply and said, 'Why does this generation ask for a miraculous sign?'" - Mark 8:12.*

Jesus sighed deeply when He asked this question. He had already done many miracles, yet the Jews wanted another sign. In their unbelief, no sign was sufficient to bring them to faith. **Is that your situation? Do you realize God has raised Jesus from the dead yet you want a sign to confirm something God wants you to do?** If God raises the dead, He can do anything and your faith has a focus that cannot be thwarted. Read Jesus' response to their request for a sign in Matthew 12:39-40, and understand you already have the sign that proves God's faithfulness and power to do anything.

# June 12: Pay Up

*"Will they not both fall into a pit?" - Luke 6:39.*

You cannot lead people where you have not gone yourself. That is one reason why the Lord has put you through some difficult trials and unusual experiences, so you will be able both to share your experience with others and also know God's goodness in times of trouble. Yet, if you don't extract the lessons from your trials, you are in some sense blind, and God cannot use you to lead, counsel, and influence others. **Are you willing to be used by God, even if it means going through painful lessons? Are you willing and able to pay the price to be effective?** Will you take the time to reflect on and learn from your life experiences? Read 1 Timothy 3:1-13 and see that all leadership comes at a price. Find your price and do whatever you have to do to pay up.

# June 13: Gifts

*"Or if he asks for a fish, will give him a snake?" - Matthew 7:10.*

A good father gives appropriate gifts to his children when they ask and even when they don't. He does not trick them or abuse their trust in his goodness as their father, but expresses his love through occasional gifts and tokens of his affection. Your perfect heavenly Father does the same, but always with your best interests in mind. **Can you trust the Father's plan for you? Do you have faith that God's provision for you at this time is His best? Can you believe that if it is not what you want at this time that it is what you need?** Read Hebrews 12:7-12 and thank God for His gifts to you in this season, even if you can't understand at the moment how they are an answer to your prayers or an expression of His love.

## June 14: You

*"But what about you?" - Matthew 16:15.*

Jesus asked the disciples what others believed and then He asked them about their own beliefs. At some point,you have to answer the question: **What about you? Are you doing what you do because your family is doing it or to please others? What about you? Are you serving the Lord because you have to or because you want to? And are you happy in what you are doing now? Do you know what you believe about Jesus and are you true to your beliefs?** Read Romans 14:4-9, and then work to be convinced of the rightness of your beliefs and actions for you and not for someone else.

## June 15: The Body

*"Who is my mother, and who are my brothers?"*
*- Matthew 12:48.*

You are part of God's family, the body of Christ, if you have put your faith in Christ. Therefore your walk is not an individual thing but a family thing. That means you have a lot of brothers and sisters and some of them can be difficult to relate to. **Are you part of a church body? Are you working at building relationships with those people in that part of God's body?** Read 1 Corinthians 12:12-31 and determine to take your place in some part of God's body.

## June 16: The Details

*"Or the seven loaves for the four thousand, and how many basketfuls you gathered?" - Matthew 16:10.*

There is an old saying that the devil is in the details. But God is in them too! In today's question, Jesus asked the disciples to remember how many baskets of food were left over when He multiplied the loaves and fish. God just doesn't provide enough; He provides in abundance. You can forget how He has provided for you and panic when things seem tight. **Are you in a provision panic now? Have you forgotten God's ability to provide?** Read Numbers 11 and see what happened to Israel when they complained about God's provision and take time to remember the details of God's goodness to you.

## June 17: Preoccupied

*"How is it you don't understand that I was not talking to you about bread?" - Matthew 16:11.*

When you are preoccupied with your own needs, it can be difficult to hear or understand what the Lord is saying to you. When that happens, even your prayer life is consumed with telling God what you need instead of listening for His voice. You can approach your own prayer life with assurance that God knows what you need, so you can then focus on other matters. **Can you accept that what you have today is what He has chosen to give you? Can you also rest in the fact that your situation may turn from lack to abundance with one phone call or meeting? Thus can you rest in the promise of His provision and seek Him for other matters like spiritual development or the needs of others?** Read what Israel did when they were consumed by their own needs in 1 Corinthians 10:1-13 and then determine not to follow their example.

## June 18: Kindness

*"And if you do good to those who are good to you, what credit is that to you?" - Luke 6:32.*

Your ethics must exceed those who do not know the Lord. Because you trust Him, you can afford to do things people perceive as "weak" or that seem to allow you to be taken advantage of. **Is there someone in your world who is not very nice to you?** Then you have the perfect chance to be kind to them even though they are not kind to you! Why? Because that is a trait like God, and when you do that you imitate Him. Plus, you are providing proof that God does exist and is working in your life. Read Proverbs 25:21- 22 and look for a chance to apply its advice today.

## June 19: A Plan

*"You, then, who teach others, do you not teach yourself?" - Romans 2:21.*

You must work to keep yourself sharp and growing in the things of the Lord. If you don't, you will begin to rely on your past or any number of other things that can command attention and compliance, but will not add to your personal growth. **What do you do that stimulates your growth? Do you read, take classes, attend seminars or engage in activities that force you to learn and grow outside of your usual routine and comfort zone?** Maybe it's time to outline a personal development plan and follow it, even if it requires you to invest money in yourself. Read 2 Peter 1:5-8 and then work out a plan to bring the increase commended in those verses.

## June 20: Stealing

*"You who preach against stealing, do you steal?" - Romans 2:21.*

There are many ways to steal that don't involve robbing a bank.

**Do you use your company's property for personal matters? Do you falsify expense reports? Do you borrow someone's tools or equipment and fail to return them in a timely manner?** Read Ephesians 4:28 and then determine that you will be above board and honest in all your dealings with the property, time, and money that belongs to someone else.

# June 21: Sexuality

*"You who say that people should not commit adultery, do you commit adultery?" - Romans 2:22.*

Jesus came to restore sexuality to its proper dignity and place, which is in marriage. Yet there are tremendous temptations today. **Are you remaining pure in this impure age? Do you have safeguards in place to insure you don't stumble? What are you willing to do if you have given in to sexual temptation?** Keep in mind that sexual sin is not to be taken lightly, but is also not an unforgiveable sin. Read 1 Corinthians 6:18-20 and do what it tells you: Flee sexual temptation and immorality.

# June 22: Idolatry

*"You who abhor idols, do you rob temples?" - Romans 2:22.*

You don't have to bow down to a statue to be involved in idolatry. Idolatry is simply putting a higher priority on anything God has created than you do on Him. Thus you can make a relationship, money, business or even your ministry an idol. What's more, you know your priorities by looking at your calendar and checkbook. **Where are your priorities? Are you worshiping God and something else also?** Read Colossians 3:5 and do what it says regarding idolatry.

# June 23: Law Breaking

*"You who brag about the law, do you dishonor God*

*by breaking the law?" - Romans 2:23.*

The Jews tried to make the Law a system to control and understand God and consequently could not recognize Jesus when He came. The Law was about a right relationship with God and others and still is. **Do you talk about the Law of God but not follow it? Do you judge others whom you consider to be breaking the Law and not adhere to it yourself?** Read Psalm 1 and evaluate how effectively you are keeping God's law which is summarized in Matthew 23:26-29.

## June 24: Generosity

*"How many loaves do you have?" - Mark 8:5.*

The disciples did not believe they could help or feed anyone else because of what they did not have. Yet Jesus taught them to use what they had and yield it to Him to obtain supernatural results. It all started by them recognizing that they didhave something they could use and give. This represented a new way of thinking that was then to lead to a new way of behaving. God wants to give you new thoughts as well which will lead to bold action on your part. **Where is your focus, on what you have or what you don't have? Are you waiting to have more before you are generous with others?** Read John 6:1-15 and see if you have been limiting your faith and not responding to needs around you. Then set your mind to use what you have to bless others.

## June 25: Self-Awareness

*"How can you say to your brother, 'Brother, let me take the speck out of your eye,' when you yourself fail to see the plank in your own eye?" - Luke 6:42.*

Self-awareness is the foundation for discipleship and leadership. You must recognize your own failures and what is going on in your heart, along with your strengths and weaknesses, if you are going to help others. You cannot empathize and assist others if you have not faced yourself. **How self-aware are you? Do you journal? Are you gentle with others realizing that you also have many weaknesses and failures?** Read Luke 15:11-24 and see how the father welcomed back his lost son when he finally came to his senses and admitted his sin. Then realize that your honesty does not disqualify you from seeking or serving God.

# June 26: Faith Level

*"O unbelieving and perverse generation," Jesus replied, "how long shall I stay with you?" - Matthew 17:17.*

Without faith it is impossible to please God. Faith is the atmosphere in which your relationship with the Lord thrives and grows. Faith is not just an event where you trust Him for certain things from time to time, but a lifestyle in which you trust Him for everything! **If you examined your life today, what would your faith level be? Are there things for which you are trusting God and, if He does not "come through," you will look foolish and fail?** Read Habakkuk 2:1-4 and see that faith was also the standard in the Old Testament and then write a faith plan and vision as the prophet suggested.

# June 27: God's Will

*"Didn't you know I had to be in my Father's house?" - Luke 2:49.*

Jesus came to do God's will, which means He knew God's will and then chose to carry it out with total commitment. Now He requires that you do the same. God's role is to reveal His will to your life, for He cannot ask you to do what you don't know or understand. Your job is to then give yourself to do His will with all the energy and strength you possess. This will is not only for the individual decisions you need to make (**Should I give this away? Should I keep quiet even though this person offended me?**) but also the decisions as to how you will spend your life fulfilling your purpose and maximizing your relationships. **Do you know God's will for your life? If you do, are you procrastinating in fear or giving everything you have to see it fulfilled? Are you growing so you can understand the implications for His will in your life?** Read Matthew 8:19-22 and then determine if there are any hindrances preventing you from following Jesus with your whole heart.

## June 28: Self-Interest

*"Would he thank the servant because he did what he was told to do?" - Luke 17:9.*

You are a servant and God is your master, and He has given you many commands to carry. When you obey, you are not doing God a favor. You are acting in your best self-interest, for your obedience enables God's blessings to shower down on your life. In other words, you don't have to do God's will, you get to do God's will. **What is your attitude these days towards obedience? Are you obeying joyfully or with a bad attitude?** Read Deuteronomy 28:1-14 and rejoice that you are able to partake in such a bounty of blessings that spring forth from your obedient relationship with Him.

## June 29: Reading

*"Have you never read . . . ?" - Mark 2:25.*

It is said that leaders are readers; but disciples of Jesus are readers too. **As you approach a new month, what are you reading? What are your reading goals? What do you do with what you learn from your reading? If you can't find time to read, can you listen to audio books?** Perhaps you can enroll in a course or program that will help direct your reading? Read Daniel 1:17 and see that God promoted the young men in Babylon in part because of their ability and devotion to learning, and then go follow their example.

# June 30: Inventory

*"But what about you?" - Matthew 16:15.*

At this halfway point of the year, it's time to do a spiritual inventory by asking yourself today's question. **What is the Spirit saying to you? Why are you doing what you are doing? Are you happy? Do you have joy? Are you doing what you are doing because you want to do it or because others want you to?** Read Daniel 6 and identify all his good spiritual practices and traits, and then pick one or two to work on with God's help for the remainder of this year.

# What Would Jesus Ask You Today?

## July

## July 1: Peace

*"Salt is good, but if it loses its saltiness, how can you make it salty again?" - Mark 9:50.*

What Jesus said after He asked this question gives you the meaning of the question: "Have salt in yourselves, and be at peace with each other." And His entire teaching was provoked when the disciples were arguing among themselves as to which of them was the greatest. Your 'salt' is to serve as a source of peace in your relationships by destroying ambition as you serve other people. **Is there anyone with whom you are estranged, with whom you once had a relationship but now do not? Has your ambition or self-centeredness caused you to compete with others or to envy who they are or what they have? Perhaps this is the day to use your salt to bring healing and peace as you serve others in love?** Read Luke 17:1-6 and then take steps today to forgive and restore peace with a friend, business associate, or family member. Read James 3:13-16 to address any selfish ambition or envy that may be affecting your relationships.

## July 2: Angry

*"Then the Lord said to Cain, 'Why are you angry?'" - Genesis 4:6.*

Anger in and of itself is not negative; it is a an emotion that God gave you to stimulate action. It's when you give in to sinful actions while angry that causes the problems. What's more, it's possible to carry long-term anger that leads to health and emotional problems. **Are you angry? How long have you been? Does it lead to sinful behavior?** Read Ephesians 4:26- 27 and remember that it's not the anger but what you do with it that is your problem. Then ask the Lord to help you with the root of your anger before it leads to other difficulties.

## July 3: Take Time

*"Jesus asked, 'Do you see anything?'" - Mark 8:23.*

It is possible to pass by things every day and not notice they are there, which includes people in all their suffering and pain. **How aware are you of the people around you? Are you so busy that you are consumed with your own needs and agenda, or can you make room today to see the reality of the world around and outside of you?** Read John 9:35-41and notice how Jesus first healed the man's physical blindness, then healed his spiritual blindness, while confronting the Pharisees concerning their own blindness. Ask God to heal you of any blindness you may have and of which you are unaware.

## July 4: Take a Stand

*"Who will rise up for me against the wicked?" - Psalm 94:16.*

All it takes for wicked people to prosper sometimes is for the righteous to do nothing. Then the profiteers of evil have no one to oppose them as they work the darkness to their advantage. **What are you doing to bring light and peace to your world? Can you help orphans, combat sex trafficking, take a stand against violence in your neighborhood or invest yourself in some other cause that promotes righteousness, without hatred or legalism?** Read this simple philosophy in Romans 12:21 and ask the Lord to show you where you can apply it in the world around you.

## July 5: The Path

*"Did not the Christ have to suffer these things and then enter his glory?" - Luke 24:26.*

Jesus' sacrifice was not an accident but rather a planned event that led to your freedom and His exaltation to the right hand of the Father. Your path to promotion and significance will follow the same pattern. **Are you suffering? Then could that be part of your preparation for God's call and purpose?** Read Philippians 2:1-11 to see how Jesus emptied Himself to be exalted and then eagerly pursue this same path to God's will for your life.

# July 6: God's Kindness

*"Or do you show contempt for the riches of his kindness, tolerance and patience, not realizing that God's kindness leads you toward repentance?" - Romans 2:4.*

Don't ever accept God's silence or blessing for His approval of certain behaviors or lifestyles. God is gracious and His kindness is not always an endorsement of your attitudes, but rather God's way of giving you time to come to your senses and repent. **How do you know whether or not your actions are out of God's will?** The first way is His word, and the second is the presence of His Spirit to convict you of sin. Are you showing contempt for God's kindness? Read John 16:8 and Psalm 119:105 and then use God's tools to determine if the need for repentance is in order.

# July 7: Lazy

*"How long will you lie there, you sluggard?" - Proverbs 6:9.*

There are some things that will only occur when you have exerted the effort and paid the price to see them happen, even if they are spiritual things. Watching television, reading trashy novels or magazines and engaging in other mindless activities will not lead to fruitfulness and are a sign of laziness that is often rooted in fear. **Are you known as a hard worker? Do you spend time on meaningful things that build you or others up?** Read Exodus 23:12 and ask if you have earned the rest of the seventh day by working hard on the other six.

# July 8: God Honoring

*"Do you not know that your body is a temple of the Holy Spirit, who is in you, whom you have received from God?" - 1 Corinthians 6:19.*

The context of this question is sexual purity. The next verse states, "You were bought at a price. Therefore honor God with your body."

The ancient Greeks tended to dismiss the body and its misdeeds as irrelevant, but believers view the body as a vital part of humanity and spirituality, thus Paul and other writers spent a great deal of time re-educating the Greek mind where the body was concerned. **Are you honoring God with your body, using it as He would like, or are you using your body (and taking care of it, for that matter) like God is not interested? Are you watching things you should not watch? Reading books you should not read?** Maintaining your sexual purity. Read 1 Corinthians 6:12-18 and then repent of any activities in which you may not be honoring God with the use of your body.

## July 9: Loud Wisdom

*"Does not wisdom call out?" - Proverbs 8:1.*

God is not hiding. He wants to make Himself known, especially to those who know Him. Therefore insight and guidance should not be a problem for you. In fact, His voice is loud and clear if you choose to hear and obey. In the book of Revelation John recorded that he heard loud voices from heaven, indicative of the fact that God's wisdom is easily accessible for those who want it. **Do you want it? Are you answering wisdom's call? Are you obeying its advice?** Read Revelation 10:1-4 and accept that heaven speaks loud and clear and all you have to do is listen and obey.

## July 10: God Envy

*"Or do you think Scripture says without reason that the spirit he caused to live in us envies intensely?" - James 4:5.*

The Spirit of God envies for you. That means He doesn't want some of you, He wants all of you. He doesn't want just your Sunday you or your Wednesday-night you. He wants the you that works and the you that relates to your family and the you that watches television and the you that goes shopping. **Have you given Him all of you? Have you surrendered to His Lordship in all areas of life? What**

**areas have yet to be surrendered?** Read 2 Chronicles 16:9 and then set your heart to be the one the Lord will find when He goes on his envious search for people who have completely surrendered to His will.

# July 11: Feedback Team

*"But who can discern their own errors?" - Psalm 19:12.*

A management expert one time said it's not that people can't fix their problems, it's that they cannot even see their problems. This is why you need to seek the honest feedback of those you trust and who love you so they can tell you what you may not be able (or willing) to see. **Who do you have in your life who can speak directly and honestly? Are you defensive when they give you feedback?** Read Psalm 141:4- 5 and then apply its truth the next time someone points out to you one of your hard-to-recognize faults or errors.

# July 12: The Great Commission

*"Why do the nations conspire and the peoples plot in vain?" - Psalm 2:1.*

Not everyone is neutral or ignorant where God is concerned. Some people hate Him, and that can be true for some nations! They despise Jesus and the Kingdom He represents. The only way to turn this around is to take the message of God's love where it is absent or opposed, and that is commonly called missions. **What are you doing to support world missions? Do you pray or give? Are you open to going to serve, short-term or long?** Read Matthew 28:19-20, which is called the Great Commission and ask God how you fit into this plan.

# July 13: Depression

*"Why, my soul, are you downcast?" - Psalm 42:11.*

There can be physical causes for depression, but it is also brought on by bad thinking. If you talked yourself into depression, then you are able to talk yourself out of it as well. **Do you battle depression? Are you depressed now?** If so, look at today's verse and see that the psalmist engaged in a conversation to talk himself out of the doldrums he was in. You can do the same. To help more read Psalm 42.

## July 14: The Rock

*"And who is the Rock except our God?" - Psalm 18:31.*

**Who is your 'rock' of life? Is it money, smarts, government or some other thing that you turn to when times are tough?** God wants to be your rock and He is a Rock for all ages and cultures. The rock in the Old Testament actually gave the people water in the desert, always present and always sufficient. Read how God provided this water in Exodus 17:1-7, and see how the people grumbled but God still provided what they needed. God is a good God!

## July 15: Strategy for Outreach

*"To what, then, can I compare the people of this generation?" - Luke 7:31.*

Jesus studied the people among whom He lived, ministered, and worshipped in order to enhance HIs teaching so He could reach them with the message of the Kingdom. What's more, He used everyday examples or descriptions to help His listeners identify where they were spiritually so they could then repent and grow in God. **How would you answer today's question for your generation or your culture, whether ethnic or national? Are they materialistic, selfish, purposeful, tribal, compliant, rebellious, lazy, or fearful?** It is important to grasp this, otherwise you will never help reach the generations if you don't understand them and their culture. Paul had a strategy to reach the people around him because he understood those people, as you can read in 1 Corinthians 9:19-23. **Are you willing to do the same for the people around you?**

# July 16: Fulfillment

*"He said, 'Do you believe in the Son of Man?'" - John 9:35.*

After Jesus healed the blind man, he asked the man if he believed in the "Son of Man." This was Jesus' favorite term for Himself and it was a direct reference to the vision Daniel had in 7:13. In other words Jesus was declaring that He was the prophetic fulfillment for Israel's Messiah! **Do you believe in Jesus?** Read Daniel 7 in its entirety and ask God to give you even deeper insight into the significance of Jesus' coming and then spread the Word that He wasn't just a prophet but a prophetic fulfillment.

# July 17: The Old

*"Why then is it written that the Son of Man must suffer much and be rejected?" - Mark 9:12.*

There is an old saying that "The New is in the Old concealed, the Old is in the New revealed. The New is in the Old contained, the Old is in the New explained." When Jesus asked this question, He only had the Old Testament as His point of reference, but pointed out many instances in the Old that described His mission and character. **How familiar are you with prophecies and references to Christ in the Old Testament?** Taking into account the importance of the Old Testament in understanding Jesus and His purpose, read what Paul said in Romans 15:3-6, and then do some reading and study to discover the treasures of Christ in the Old Testament.

# July 18: Finish Well

*"Do you not know that in a race all the runners run, but only one gets the prize?" - 1 Corinthians 9:24.*

Your Christian walk is a marathon, not a sprint. The goal is both to compete and to finish well. Much of what you are asked to do will only have long-term returns that require faith and patience. **Are you**

**running the race well? Are you determined to 'win' while competing by the rules, so to speak?** Read Galatians 6:7-10 and then set your heart to do things that will please the Lord and allow you to finish well as you serve Him.

## July 19: Easy

*"Which is easier: to say to the paralytic, 'Your sins are forgiven,' or to say, 'Get up, take your mat and walk'?" - Mark 2:9.*

God accomplishes His will by His word. He speaks and things happen. Thus the answer to today's question is that neither one is easier for God; both are possible just by and through His word. **So, are you struggling with forgiveness?** God says that you are forgiven and you can take that to the bank! **Do you need healing?** God is able to speak a word and your body will be healed. Read Isaiah 55:8-13 to comprehend the power of God's words, and then walk in the faith that those words are as powerful for and in you as for anyone else.

## July 20: Credit

*"And if you lend to those from whom you expect repayment, what credit is that to you?" - Luke 6:34.*

Jesus encouraged His followers to store up treasure in heaven by doing things that only the Father can reward them for doing. One of them was giving and lending to those from whom you expect no return. God Himself gives to those who do not even acknowledge His existence and it is a godly trait to be generous just like He is. **Are you freely giving? Are you giving with any expectation of benefit or reward from the recipient?** Read Deuteronomy 15:9-11 and see how God commanded you to be generous even though it may cost you to do so and then gain no credit with God for doing it.

# July 21: Strategy

*"Who will take a stand for me against evildoers?"*
*- Psalm 94:16.*

Edmund Burke once said, "All that is necessary for the triumph of evil is that good men do nothing." It isn't enough to complain about evil or pray against evil; you must actively oppose it in your community and nation. At the same time, you must not be angry but do what Gandhi said, "Hate the sin, love the sinner." **Against what evil are you taking a stand? How are you doing it? Where should you get involved?** A possible strategy to combat evil is found in Romans 12:20-21. Read it and see where you can apply it today.

# July 22: Wake Up!

*"When will you get up from your sleep?" - Proverbs 6:9.*

Fear and laziness will always motivate you to put off doing what is in your heart until tomorrow, next month. or next year. If you are not careful, you will begin to believe how you spin why you are not doing something, excuses such as "I am waiting on the Lord," or "It's not the right time or season" or "I'm praying about it." What's more, don't talk about what you will do in the future as if your future is guaranteed, when today may be your last day on earth. **Are you procrastinating? Why? What can you do to wake up and get moving?** Read Genesis 22:1-3 and see that Abraham set out early in the morning to do God's will; you should have the same attitude.

# July 23: Fear

*"The Lord is my light and my salvation—*
*whom shall I fear?" - Psalm 27:1.*

Fear is the greatest obstacle to a life of faith, productivity and purpose. You can fear failure, criticism, other people, success, God and just about anything else that you encounter in life. This condition is a carryover from the Garden for, when Adam and Eve sinned, they hid from God in shame and fear. John wrote that love casts out fear. So in some sense your fear is really a deficiency of your love relationship with the Lord (see 1 John 4:18). **Where are the fears in your life?** Read 2 Timothy 1:7 and then work to face and overcome your fears that are keeping you from God's best.

## July 24: Quickly

*"How long, Lord, how long?" - Psalm 6:3.*

In Luke 18:7-8, Jesus promised God would administer justice and do it quickly. The problem is that His definition of quickly and yours may be off by quite a large margin. Your idea may be days, His idea weeks. You may think quickly is months and He may be thinking years. **Are you currently waiting for some breakthrough or victory the Lord has promised? Does it seem like you have been waiting a long time, longer than you expected? Are you discouraged or even disillusioned?** Determine today to align your expectations with God's and put it all in His hands to carry out His promises as 'quickly' as He deems appropriate.

## July 25: Honest with God

*"Why do you hide yourself in times of trouble?" - Psalm 10:1.*

The men who wrote the psalms were honest with God. They said things to God that were on their heart, even if they questioned God's motives and love! Of course as they did, they saw the real truth—that God is faithful and loving, and their perceptions of Him were often less than perfect. **Are you honest with God? Do you tell God what you think He wants to hear or what is really going on in your mind and heart?** Read Psalm 18:25-29 and see that God responds and relates to you as you do to Him.

## July 26: Prosperity

*"Many, Lord, are asking, 'Who will bring us prosperity?'" - Psalm 4:6.*

Your company does not support you, nor do your investments or the government. The Lord uses them, but He is ultimately the One who takes care of you. **Where is your focus? Is it on your ability to invest, in your bimonthly paycheck or in your pension?** If it is on any of those, look and consider again that it all comes from Him. Therefore you should put your trust in Him and not anyone or anything else. Read Proverbs 11:28 and then do a simple search of the word "riches" in Proverbs to see what else you can learn and apply.

## July 27: Desert Provision

*"Can God really spread a table in the wilderness?" - Psalm 78:19.*

God is not limited by a poor economy or other conditions. He can provide for you and do it abundantly in any circumstances. Where there is lack, either God is testing you for a season or else your expectation may be too small. God spread a table in the desert and fed millions of people for years; He can do the same for you and yours. **Are you limiting God by your wrong thinking? Is your focus on the "desert conditions" or on God?** Read Psalm 78:20-31 to see what God did in response to today's question, and then determine not to be like those who were asking it.

## July 28: Involvement

*"Dear woman, why do you involve me?" - John 2:4.*

Mary involved Jesus in the wine shortage at the wedding feast, and He performed His first public miracle. You are part of the body of Christ, so you carry Him with you wherever you go. He expects you to involve Him not just in church, but in all your world, whether business, family, school or neighborhood. You can do this through prayer, witnessing and applying His Word and principles to your expressions of life. **Are you involving Jesus in all you do? How can you involve Him even more?** Read Colossians 3:22-25 and apply it to today's verse by reflecting God in all you do and say.

# July 29: High View

*"Has not Moses given you the law?" - John 7:19.*

Jesus acknowledged that Moses delivered the Law to Israel and wrote the first books of the Bible. That contradicts some modern theologians who dispute Moses' authorship, as well as that of other biblical writers. **If Jesus took a 'high' view of Scripture, don't you think you should as well? If God's Word is inspired and accurate as Jesus maintained, then how often do you read it and then do you make it your standard for life and behavior?** Read Mark 12:18-27 and notice how Jesus referred to the Scriptures and pointed out how trained and educated men in Israel had misunderstood them. That is the reason you also need to rely on Jesus through the Spirit to interpret the Bible and also guide your application of its truth.

# July 30: Interpretation

*"How do you read it?" - Luke 10:26.*

Jesus question today was really an attempt to ask, "How do you interpret or understand it?" The "it" refers to Scripture. The rules you use to interpret Scripture will determine what you do with what you read, so it's important to have some basic guidelines. One such rule is to "let Scripture interpret Scripture" wherever possible. Another is to study everything on a particular topic so that one verse does not become an end unto itself. **Do you have any rules for interpretation? If not, is it time that you read or took a course to help you identify some?** Read 2 Peter 3:14-18 and determine not to distort the Scriptures as Peter said is the habit of some.

# July 31: Honest To God

*"How long will you defend the unjust and show partiality to the wicked?" - Psalm 82:2.*

Many of the psalmists questioned God's faithfulness as they

considered how the wicked prospered and the righteous suffered. It was important that they were honest with God, for then He was honest with them. Their psalms may have started questioning God, but they all ended praising Him. **Are you being honest with God? Are you denying the truth that you sometimes question His deeds or His speed in responding to your needs?** Be honest with Him, but then be ready for God to respond and be honest with you. Only then can your perspective be cleared so you can see things from God's point of view and not just your own. Read Psalm 82 in its entirety and see if you can determine who is speaking and what the lesson is, and then seek to emulate its directness and transparency before God.

# What Would Jesus Ask You Today?

## August

## August 1: The Basics

*"And why do you worry about clothes" - Matthew 6:28.*

The question can be expanded to ask, "Why do you worry about anything at all?" God is able to provide for all your needs, including food, shelter, transportation and even relationships. **So why spend any time and energy at all worrying about your basic needs? Has God ever failed you? Are you enjoying His blessings or worrying about the future? Is worry a sinful habit that you need to correct with the Spirit's help?** Read Ecclesiastes 2:17-26 and apply its conclusions to your life today.

## August 2: Foundations

*"When the foundations are being destroyed, what can the righteous do?" - Psalm 11:3.*

Many are concerned because of the shaking going on in the world. Perhaps you are one of them. There is only one thing you can do in perilous or changing times, and that is to make sure your own foundation in the Lord is firm and that you have an accurate picture of who God is. **Is your faith shaken these days? Are you concerned about the course of history and culture in this generation?** Read Psalm 11 in its entirety and secure an adequate picture of God's power as He sits on His throne in heaven. Then make sure your foundations in the Lord are strong.

## August 3: Hiding

*"But the Lord God called to the man, 'Where are you?'" - Genesis 3:9.*

Adam and Eve hid from the Lord after they sinned, and mankind has been hiding ever since. They hid because of guilt and shame ,and those two motivators still cause us to hide from God and one another. **Are you hiding? Of what are you ashamed? Of what are you**

**afraid?** If you can face your fears and shame, you can overcome them. But if you continue to hide, you will never be free. Read Matthew 25:14-30 and see what fear caused one of the stewards to do. Then reflect on what fear is causing you to do (and lose) in your life.

## August 4: Both

*"Which is easier: to say, 'Your sins are forgiven,' or to say, 'Get up and walk'?" - Luke 5:23.*

Jesus summed it up best when he said, "What is impossible with man is possible with God" (Luke 18:27). Both healing and forgiveness of sins are miracles, yet God accomplishes both with ease and grace. **Do you need healing? Then ask and seek the Lord. Do you need forgiveness?** Then ask and receive. Read Isaiah 53:4-6 and understand that Jesus' mission was not to provide one or the other, but both healing and forgiveness. Then determine to make both an important part of your life and walk.

## August 5: Travel

*"If not, what did you go out to see?" - Luke 7:25.*

In this verse, Jesus asked His audience why so many of them traveled to see John the Baptist for spiritual reasons. People today still go out to seek entertainment at movies, sporting events, concerts, and other places. There they connect with others, take their minds off their other duties, and look for a reprieve from the pressures of life. There is nothing wrong with that as long as the entertainment is moral and wholesome. **Yet if you go out to be socially connected and entertained, shouldn't you also travel to be spiritually fed and stimulated like the Jews did when they went to see John? Is there a conference you go to that 'feeds' your soul?** Is there a speaker you will travel to see? Read Deuteronomy 16:13-17 to see that travel for spiritual reasons was part of God's agenda for His people then. **If that is still true today, where will you go?**

## August 6: Words

*"Now my heart is troubled, and what shall I say?"*
*- John 12:27.*

When you are sad, anxious, angry or depressed, it is important to control your words, both in your mind and your mouth. At that point, your thoughts can either help you get out of your funk or put you deeper in a pit. The words you speak will either lift you up or bring you down; allow people to get close to help or push them away. **Do you believe your words affect your mood and can either make your condition better or worse?** Proverbs has many things to say about words and the tongue, but for today read Proverbs 21:23.

## August 7: Mere Mortals

*"What can mere mortals do to me?" - Psalm 56:4.*

Mere mortals can criticize, persecute, ostracize, ignore, and do physical or financial damage. That's what they can do! That is why it is so easy to fear them, which speaks to the importance of learning to trust the Lord for protection and provision. **Are you fearing what "mere mortals" can do to you? What is this fear costing you in terms of being who God wants you to be and doing what He wants?** Read the entire verse here and then reflect on what Jesus said in Luke 12:1-12 to see how it applies to your life.

## August 8: Help

*"I lift up my eyes to the hills—*
*where does my help come from" - Psalm 121:1.*

The hills around Jerusalem were not adequate to protect the psalmist. Instead he came to the conclusion that his help came from the Lord. Your help does not come from your business smarts, your money, your family name or your insurance company. Like the psalmist, your help comes from the Lord, whether you realize it or not. **In what**

**or whom have you put your confidence and placed your trust?** Read Psalm 33:16- 19, and then assess how you will answer today's question.

## August 9: Your Cross

*"'But what about you?' he asked" - Luke 9:20.*

You cannot live off someone else's faith. At some point Jesus will get specific, and you will face a crisis or faith challenge that will test your own relationship with the Lord. You must also follow the path God has for you and not the one He has for someone else. **Do you know what you believe? More importantly, do you know the One in whom you believe?** Read Matthew 10:37-39 and then meditate on whether or not you are carrying your cross, or watching someone else carry theirs.

## August 10: Times of Testing

*"How long, Lord?" - Psalm 13:1.*

When you are going through a trial or time of testing, it doesn't seem like it will ever end. Yet they all do, and yours is no exception. **Are you going through a tough time? Is that the question you are asking today?** No one knows the answer but the Lord, and He may not be letting you in on it! So it is best that you take it one day at a time and trust that God is working out His plan in the midst of your pain. Read Psalm 56:8-11 and come to the same conclusion that the psalmist came to in the midst of his time of tears.

## August 11: Characteristics

*"Lord, who may dwell in your sacred tent?" - Psalm 15:1.*

Of course God does not live in a tent but, at the time of the psalmist, the ark of the covenant was set up in one and the people came there to worship. So the question could also be phrased, "**What are your**

**requirements for worship?"** While you cannot earn the right to worship, you must maintain a right heart and actions to continue to worship. Paul described the characteristics he expected from believers in all his letters, and you can read part of his instruction in Philippians 3:15-21. **Are you manifesting these characteristics?**

## August 12: The Kingdom

*"How then can his kingdom stand?" - Matthew 12:26.*

The truth is that no kingdom apart from God's kingdom can or will stand. Therefore, you are wise if you devote your time and energy to build His kingdom, which is something that has eternal value. That does not mean you have to work in church, but rather learn how to extend God's rule and reign in any area of life, like family, business, education, or culture. **Are you building your own kingdom or God's? How can you tell the difference (usually it has to with serving others or serving self)? Is there something more you can do to apply Kingdom principles to your life or work?** As added incentive to invest your energy in the Kingdom, read Hebrews 12:25-29.

## August 13: Foretold

*"David himself calls him 'Lord.'*
*How then can he be his son?" - Mark 12:37.*

The psalms all point toward a Messiah King who was yet to come save His people and, of course, that King was and is Jesus. Not only the psalmists but also all the Old Testament writers looked forward to Jesus who is the fulfillment of Old Testament prophecy and promises. **How familiar are you with the Old Testament? What are you doing to grow in your understanding? Have you misapplied any Old Testament passages to anything but the ministry and work of Christ?** Read Romans 1:1-3 and see that the gospel was certainly foretold in the Old Testament; then go back and see if you can find where!

# August 14: Doing God a Favor

*"Do I eat the flesh of bulls or drink the blood of goats?"*
*- Psalm 50:13.*

Some in Israel got to the point where they thought they were doing God a favor when they offered sacrifices to Him. We can have the same attitude when we give or obey. When you think you are doing God a favor when we do his will, however, we can have high expectations of a reward or a smug feeling of self-righteousness. Yet our obedience is not for God's sake; it is for ours. **Has this attitude crept into your obedience? Are you disappointed when God doesn't reward you as you think He should when you do His will?** Read Luke 17:7-10 and Hebrews 10:32-39, and be reminded of your role as God's servant, not His equal.

# August 15: Rights

*"What right have you to recite my laws or*
*take my covenant on your lips" - Psalm 50:16.*

You don't have any rights with God, but He bestows privileges and honors when you put your trust in Jesus for salvation. If you think you have rights, however, you will conclude at times that God is not treating you fairly, and may even believe the lie that He is unjust or whimsical. **Are you standing for your rights in the Lord or relying on His grace and mercy? If it the latter, are you being merciful yourself to others?** Take a look at Job 40 and then see if any of Job's attitudes have seeped into your own relationship with the Lord.

# August 16: The Gentle Jesus

*"Shall I come to you with a whip,*
*or in love and with a gentle spirit?" - 1 Corinthians 4:21.*

Jesus came with a whip both to those who made the Temple a business enterprise and to those who were self-righteous. He came with a gentle spirit to those caught in sin, recognized that fact and sought Him humbly and gladly. If you want to meet the gentle Jesus, then you should approach Him in the same manner with the same attitude. **Are you judgmental of others caught in some sin? Are you aware of your shortcomings? Do you confess your sins regularly?** Luke 19:1-10 shows an example of this very principle.

## August 17: Your Brain

*"Do you not know that we will judge angels?"*
*- 1 Corinthians 6:3.*

When Jesus returned from the dead, He had full memory of what had happened in his lifetime. Your brain is the only organ that keeps developing and does not grow "old." The point is that what you learn now you will carry with you into the next life ,and you will obviously use it in some capacity. **So what are you doing to keep growing and learning? What are you doing to sharpen your spiritual discernment and wisdom? Have you retired from the work of personal development?** Read the context of today's question in 1 Corinthians 6:1-6 and then get ready to judge the world eventually.

## August 18: Tasty

*"Salt is good, but if it loses its saltiness,*
*how can it be made salty again?" - Luke 14:34.*

You are to be salt and light in any situation in which the Lord places you. **The light is fairly obvious, but what about the salt?** You are to make others thirsty to know more about the Lord. You are to preserve situations through your integrity and holiness. And you are to provide a tasty treat to every situation by being agreeable and positive. **Are you ready to accept your duties as the salt of the earth? Have you lost some of your flavor, no longer tasty but leaving a sour or bittertaste in others?** A good example of this is the account of Paul's presence on the ship to Rome in Acts 27. Determine to be like him in your own storms of life.

# August 19: Diligence

*"How long will you lie there, you sluggard?"*
*- Proverbs 6:9.*

Success is never a mistake or an accident. It is always the result of hard work and diligence coupled with God's blessing. You can envy what someone else has done, or you can decide if God did it for them, He can do it for you. With that latter attitude, you are motivated to pay the price and never give up as you pursue your goals and dreams. **Are you wishing for success but not willing to pay the price for it? Are you immobilized because you have seen someone else's success and don't see how you can do the same? Are you looking for a shortcut in order to achieve your dreams?** Read Psalm 1 to see what you must do first and foremost to enjoy God's favor and success. Then take a look at this list from Proverbs that speak about diligence to see what you can learn from them.

# August 20: Testimony

*"Who can proclaim the mighty acts of the Lord*
*or fully declare his praise?" - Psalm 106:2.*

The answer is no one can adequately declare God's goodness, but that doesn't mean we should stop trying to tell others what God has done for us, while we are also praising Him for His goodness. **When is the last time you gave a testimony to someone about God's goodness? If you can't speak it, can you write it in a letter or email, or post it somewhere online? Is your praise and worship more expressive and mature today than in earlier days because of your growing appreciation for God's work in your life?** Read Revelation 12:10-12 and see that your testimony and praise have power to defeat your enemy and strengthen your spiritual walk and life.

# August 21: Stronghold

*"The Lord is the stronghold of my life—*

*of whom shall I be afraid?" - Psalm 27:1.*

A stronghold is a place you run into and take refuge when you are under attack. Is the Lord the stronghold in your life? Don't answer too quickly. **If He is, then why are you still afraid? In fact, are you even aware that you are afraid?** Identify what it is that you are afraid of, and then find out how you can make the Lord your stronghold in that area so fear will no longer rule in your mind. Read Psalm 56:2-4 and determine to walk out its declaration in your life in all situations in which you find fear trying to gain the upper hand.

## August 22: God's Care

*"O Lord, what is man that you care for him,*
*the son of man that you think of him?" - Psalm 144:3.*

The Lord takes care of you. Even if things are not going well for you right now, think how much worse they could be if the Lord was not watching out for you! And if things are going well, then praise and thank Him as the Source of all good things! **Can you thank the Lord for His care, even if you are struggling? Can you take time in the midst of your prosperity to acknowledge Him?** Read all of Psalm 144 to see the context in which David wrote those words, and notice that he prayed it in the midst of his enemies!

## August 23: The Tree

*"Have you eaten from the tree that I commanded you*
*not to eat from?" - Genesis 3:11.*

Yes, Adam and Eve ate from the tree of the knowledge of good and evil. That gave them the tendency to judge for themselves what is right and wrong instead of relying on God's word. That trait is still part of your makeup, which makes it easy to say, "I don't think there is anything wrong with this or that," or "It's not my fault!" **Do you rely more on feelings rather than a standard of behavior to determine right and wrong? Do you justify what you did instead**

**of saying, "I was wrong"?** 2 Samuel 12:1-13 shows David's response when confronted with his sin; you should respond the same way.

## August 24: The Price

*"What did you go out into the desert to see?" - Matthew 11:9.*

The people went to great pains to visit John the Baptist in the desert regions to see if he was the Messiah, or if he had a word from the Lord. They were waiting expectantly for God to move, and they were actively seeking His will and purpose to the point of personal discomfort and distance. **What price are you willing to pay to learn what God is doing and be a part of it? Are you active or passive where the things of God are concerned?** Read Exodus 23:14-17 and see what price the men of Israel had to pay to appear before the Lord every year.

## August 25: The Cover

*"But what did you go out to see" - Luke 7:26.*

John the Baptist was a strange fellow, with an unusual outfit and diet! Yet God chose him to prepare the way, and all Israel went to check him out. It is easy to judge someone by their exterior and determine whether or not he or she can be used of God. **Are you judging people right now by how they look or any other personal preference?** You may be missing what God has in store for you because you are judging a book by its cover, as the old saying goes. Read Isaiah 53:1-3 and see that God can hide His treasures in plain packaging, as was the case with Jesus Himself.

## August 26: A Narrow View

*"Or haven't you read in the Law that on the Sabbath the priests in the temple desecrate the day and yet are innocent?" - Matthew 12:5.*

It is an interesting phenomenon that the more Bible one knows, the meaner and more legalistic the reader can become! For example, the Pharisees took a narrow, legalistic view of Scripture and it caused them to miss the more important values therein, like love, mercy, and grace. They set up a system of rules to undergird the Law that became oppressive and rigid, and they were adding to that system all the time. **What has Scripture done for and to you? Has it made you more compassionate or more legalistic? As you grow in your understanding, do you grow in grace? Do you spend time reading the Word to allow it to transform you, or is it only to become familiar with the stories and content?** Read Luke 11:41-54 and ask the Lord to show you if you adopted the approach the Pharisees took in any area of life or biblical study.

## August 27: Unity

*"If Satan is divided against himself, how can his kingdom stand?" - Luke 11:18.*

Unity of purpose is a powerful tool for any team. That is why God is so clear that you must do all you can to preserve the unity in the Body, and that is why the enemy is so determined to wreck that unity. **Are you a source of unity or discord? How can you be an agent of reconciliation, harmony and unity?** Read Matthew 18:19 and see the power that is inherent when just a few are united in purpose and pray. Then go find some likeminded believers and release that power in unity.

## August 28: Questions

*"If then David calls him 'Lord,' how can he be his son?" - Matthew 22:45.*

Jesus asked many questions when He was teaching to help people understand His points. This helped them come to their own conclusions as opposed to Him imposing answers on them. Someone once said that quality questions lead to a quality life. Even Jesus did this, as you can see in Luke 2:45-46. **If this was His style of learning and teaching, don't you think it should be yours as well?**

## August 29: Your Business

*"If I want him to remain alive until I return, what is that to you? You must follow me." - John 21:22.*

You must learn to mind your own spiritual business and not meddle in the affairs of others. That means not comparing how God is working in the life of another as compared to yours, or trying to follow or imitate His plan for the life of another. You have your own path of discipleship to walk and walk it you must, regardless of what others do or God does for them. **Are you minding your own spiritual business? Are you busy finding your own cross and carrying it, or are you fretting about what others are or are not doing?** Make it your goal to do what Jesus commanded in Matthew 16:23-25.

## August 30: Your Brothers

*"Where is your brother Abel?" - Genesis 4:9.*

The Lord asked Cain where his brother was after Cain had killed him. Cain was evasive with his answer. Do you know where you brothers are? To answer, you have to be part of a church body and know who your brothers and sisters are. Then you must pay attention to their needs and condition, so you can answer this question on their behalf when the Lord asks you. **Are you part of a regular fellowship group? Are you working to have close relationships so you can know the needs of the people in that group?** Read Hebrews 10:24-25 and make sure you heed its warning not to separate yourself from others.

## August 31: Growing

*"Who is this King of glory?" - Psalm 24:8.*

Today's question is one that should have an ongoing, evolving answer. The God you serve today is hopefully not the God you served last year. God doesn't change, but your understanding of Him hopefully does change for the better. You should know Him better and appreciate Him more than you have at any time in the past. **Have your devotion, adoration and appreciation for the Lord grown over time? Are they still becoming deeper and richer?** Read Jeremiah 9:23-24 and make it your aim and boast that you know the Lord more and more, better and better as time goes on.

# What Would Jesus Ask You Today?

## September

## September 1: Yourself

*"How do you know, wife, whether you will save your husband?" - 1 Corinthians 7:16.*

You have no control over others, nor can you change anyone else. This pertains to your spouse, children and people closest to you. That is why your best approach is to work on you and you alone, while you teach, pray for and love others. **Are you frustrated that you cannot change someone else? Are you spending more time and energy focusing on yourself or on the adjustments others need to make?** Read Titus 3:3-8 and see what you should be teaching others, which is also to be your the standard of behavior.

## September 2: The Rules

*"Do you not know that in a race all the runners run, but only one gets the prize?" - 1 Corinthians 9:24.*

The Christian walk is a long-distance marathon, not a sprint. You will have ups and downs, but the important thing is that you keep on learning and growing from your mistakes and experiences. What's more, you must run according to the "rules," which are the commandments and directives contained in God's word. **Are you running your race well? Are you running according to the rules?** Read John 14:21 and notice the benefit for you if you show your love for God by obeying His commands.

## September 3: Sexual Purity

*"Can a man scoop fire into his lap without his clothes being burned?" - Proverbs 6:27.*

There are always implications for sin and this question pertains to adultery and sexual impropriety. Proverbs and Paul both focus on this topic and in these days, this message of purity is more relevant than ever. **Are you maintaining your sexual purity these days?**

**Are your relationships clean and righteous? Are your eyes focusing on healthy images or impure ones?** Read the verses leading up to this question in Proverbs 6:20-26 and do what you must to follow its advice.

## September 4: Prophecy

*"The Sovereign Lord has spoken—*
*who can but prophesy?" - Amos 3:8.*

God is always speaking to His people, but of course never in a manner that contradicts His word. Yet there are those who speak on His behalf to help God's people understand what it is He is doing in their lives and in the life of the church. This is called prophecy. The Bible warns not to despise prophecy, but to judge it to insure it is sound and biblical. **What is God speaking into your life right now? What is He speaking at your church fellowship?** Read 1 Corinthians 14:26-33 and see that God wishes to speak through His servants in such a way that people know they have heard from Him. Is that dynamic present in your life?

## September 5: Angry

*"Is it right for you to be angry?" - Jonah 4:4.*

The Bible never says not to be angry because anger is a natural human emotion. It does, however, advise you to control and deal with your anger, allowing it to motivate you to correct and not sinful action. In this context, Jonah was angry because the Lord had dissolved a vine that was giving Jonah shade. Yet the Lord owned the vine, so to speak, and could do with it whatever He chose, so Jonah's anger was inappropriate. **Are you angry over something about which you have no right to be upset? Are you angry over some legitimate issue, such as an injustice or wrong done to you or others? How long have you been carrying this anger? Isn't it time to confront and deal with it, whether legitimate or not? What appropriate action can your anger motivate you to take?** Read

Ecclesiastes 7:8-9 and Ephesians 4:26-27, and then follow the advice given about anger.

## September 6: Burdened

*"My people, what have I done to you? How have I burdened you?" - Micah 6:3.*

It is not a burden to serve the Lord. In fact, it is more of a burden not to! You don't have to do what He commands, you get to obey, and that has great benefits. Therefore, you must never act like you are doing God a favor when you follow Him and obey His commands. **Is serving the Lord a burden in any area? Do you rejoice in your chances to follow and obey? Do you have any heart areas that are not rejoicing which you need to confront and seek His help to change?** Jeremiah 15:15-21 shows what the Lord said to someone who was acting like it was a burden to follow Him.

## September 7: Involvement

*"Is it a time for you yourselves to be living in your paneled houses, while this house remains a ruin?" - Haggai 1:3.*

Today God's house is not a building, but His church, for which Jesus gave His life. Your gifts and time are to be used, at least in part, to help establish His church where you are a part. **Are you involved? Are you giving what He gave you to build up His body locally and through the world?** Read Romans 12:3-8 to understand your role in building His body and ask the Lord how you can invest yourself.

## September 8: Light and Dark

*"Or what fellowship can light have with darkness?" - 2 Corinthians 6:14.*

This question makes the point that believers must be careful when dealing with unbelievers. The believer and unbeliever better have the same values or it will be unproductive and painful. **Do you have relationships where you are pulling in a different direction as an unbeliever involved? Can you break it off to keep your holiness and sanctity? Does this mean to have nothing to do with unbelievers?** Read Paul's clarification on this in 1 Corinthians 5:9-11.

## September 9: History

*"Has anything like this ever happened in your days or in the days of your ancestors?" - Joel 1:2.*

God did not start working or moving in your generation. He has been at work in the hearts and minds of men for thousands of years. It is a good thing not only to know the history in the Bible, but also church history since the Bible was written and then preached and applied to life and culture. **How aware are you of church history? Do you know what God has done and how He has moved throughout the centuries? Can you apply any lessons of church history to your walk and work today?** Read Nehemiah 8 and see how Israel celebrated a festival at which time they did nothing but read the history of God's work among them, and how it impacted their lives. Perhaps you should also spend some time learning more about how God has moved in the past in order to appreciate where you are in Him today.

## September 10: His Anger

*"Who can withstand his indignation? Who can endure his fierce anger?" - Nahum 1:6.*

Of course, the answer to these questions is "No one!" It is difficult to think of God being angry because human anger is often tainted by sin. Yet God does become angry and not sin, and therefore it is wise to avoid those things that move Him to anger, like pride, rebellion and stubbornness. Read Mark 3:4-6 and then ask yourself: **What made Jesus angry there? Are these traits part of my life and walk with Him? Do I need to repent of the same attitudes the Jews had?**

## September 11: Good Things

*"Is it not from the mouth of the Most High that both calamities and good things come?" - Lamentations 3:38.*

The writer of this question was in the midst of massive upheaval in Judea as God dealt with His people for their rebellion and sin. Yet God's discipline was motivated by love and compassion to turn the people back to the Lord and His Law, which was the only way they could thrive and prosper. It says in Hebrews 12:4-6 that God disciplines us like a Father. **Are you going through a tough or painful time, perhaps feeling like the Lord is disciplining you?** Allow the discipline to have its purposed result and trust that God will once again bring 'good times' back to you and yours.

## September 12: Robbing

*"Will a mere mortal rob God? Yet you rob me."*
*- Malachi 3:8.*

The prophet was referring to people who don't give God His due by not acknowledging His Lordship over their finances through generous giving. In the Old Testament, people gave to the Temple and synagogue to support God's work and workers; today, they are to give to His church and the poor. When you do that, you are actually giving to Him; when you don't, you are withholding from Him. **Are you paying your dues, so to speak, to your local church so it can carry on its ministry? Are you giving some of what you have to those who have less or nothing?** Read Matthew 25:31-46 and then assess whether or not you are robbing or giving to God.

## September 13: His Return

*"Why do you stand here looking into the sky?"*
*- Acts 1:11.*

Many have become rich over fictional renditions of things that are not clear in the Bible; yet they portray themselves as experts on the end times. Your focus is to be your work on earth and not idle speculations about what will happen when the end comes and Jesus returns. **Are you infatuated with the things to come or the things happening now? Are you working to please the Lord today and trusting He will take care of tomorrow?** Read 2 Thessalonians 2 and focus on what Paul says to do now, realizing that his teaching on the Lord's return is not clear and predictable as some make it out to be.

## September 14: Fasting

*". . . Was it really for me that you fasted?"*
*- Zechariah 7:5.*

Fasting is an essential spiritual discipline, but one that is tough to embrace. Your flesh likes to be fed and will rebel when it is not. **When is the last time you fasted? If you did, what was your purpose in doing so? Was it to seek the Lord? For health reasons? Because others were doing it along with you? If it's been a while, why is that?** Read Isaiah 58 about what the Lord calls "true fasting," and then determine to make fasting a regular part of your spiritual routine.

## September 15: Honest Prayer

*"My God, my God, why have you forsaken me?"*
*- Psalm 22:1.*

Jesus quoted this psalm while on the cross. What honesty at a time when He was suffering most! Yet the rest of this psalm is a statement of steadfast faith and hope in God. **How honest is your prayer life? Are you telling God what you think He wants you to say, or are you pouring out your heart?** God cannot bring you to where you want to be until you admit where you are! Read Hebrews 4:14-17, and see that Jesus was like you in every way, except sin, and He can relate to your suffering and confusion. Don't hide the reality of where you are from the Lord, or from others for that matter.

# September 16: Unfaith

*"How long shall I stay with you and put up with you?"*
*- Luke 9:41.*

Jesus asked this question as He responded to His disciples' lack of faith when they could not minister healing to a young boy. This incident occurred shortly after He had first revealed to them that He would be put to death by the authorities, so perhaps their faith in His person had taken a hit and they weren't quite sure what to think or do. Jesus immediately identified the problem and let His displeasure be known. Since faith pleases God, 'un-faith' must displease Him, as evidenced by Jesus' reaction here. **Are you walking in faith, trusting God for great things? Has your faith been shaken or challenged by some event you never thought could or would happen as a believer? Or do your actions and your words portray a display of faith or a dismal pessimism concerning some issue or life in general?** Read Hebrews 10:36-39 and then decide if you are among those pressing forward in faith or shrinking back in fear.

# September 17: False Gods

*"How long will you love delusions and seek false gods?"*
*- Psalm 4:2.*

There are those who have a graven image and bow down to it as a god, but there are also mental images of false gods that are just as powerful and dangerous. It is idolatrous to worship God as you want Him to be and not according to the truth of who He really is. It is also idolatry to make relationships, money, fame or success a higher priority than the pursuit of God. **Are you ready to have God show you any religious delusions in your mind? Are you worshipping the Lord or His creation?** Read Ephesians 5:6-11 and ask if something or someone has taken His rightful priority in your life.

# September 18: Faith Thoughts

*"If that is how God clothes the grass of the field, which is here*

*today and tomorrow is thrown into the fire, will he not much more clothe you, O you of little faith?" - Matthew 6:30.*

There is no need to worry about your provision, for God has promised to take care of you. When you fret and worry, it's not just a bad habit--it's sinful behavior. When you worry, you are in essence thinking, "I wonder if I will starve or go without something? I'm not sure if God cares or is able to provide." And that, quite simply, is fear generated by lack of faith. **Are you in a state of anxiety over your job, clothes, bills, future, or health?** If you are, you don't have to live like that. With God's help, you can stop the worry and focus on faith, not doubt. Read Leviticus 25:1-22 and see how God was able to promise His provision, even when He commanded the people not to work while they lived in the harshest conditions. He will do the same for you in every situation. Once you grasp that truth, you will be able to replace worry thoughts with faith thoughts.

## September 19: Family Members

*"'Men, you are brothers; why do you want to hurt each other?'" - Acts 7:26.*

This is the question Moses asked Jews who were fighting, but the same question can be asked of believers today. You are part of the family of God; that makes your fellow believers also your brothers and sisters. You should therefore be looking for ways to bless and serve your family members, not for ways to hurt and malign them. **How well are you getting along with God's family at this point in time? What can you do to enhance your relationships in the body of Christ? Are they a priority and focus for your acts of kindness and service?** Read Hebrews 13:1-8, and apply one of its lessons to your church family relationships today.

## September 20: Committed Hearts

*"Don't you see that nothing that enters a person*

*from the outside can defile them?" - Mark 7:18.*

This question represented a major change for the Jews, for they were convinced that certain foods and actions would contaminate them and render them useless for God's service and worship. Jesus was here indicating that it was the heart that made a person unclean, not jewelry, food or clothing. **Are you focusing on externals or the heart? Are you more concerned with what things look like than how things actually are on the inside?** 1 Samuel 16:7 reminds you that God is looking for committed hearts and not just those who focus on external appearances.

## September 21: Church Work

*"Who authorized you to rebuild this temple and to finish it?" - Ezra 5:3.*

The builders of the Temple had opponents, and those who build the church of Jesus Christ have theirs. Since church work is the most important work there is, you can expect fierce opposition from the enemies of the Church. Just because Jesus said the gates of hell won't prevail against the church does not indicate that hell won't try to prevail. **Are you discouraged with your local church?** That's part of the warfare! **Do you want to just stay home and not participate?** That is too! See Revelation 12 as the symbolism of the ongoing friction between God and His enemies. Then be encouraged to know that in the end He wins, along with those who serve Him.

## September 22: Partnership

*"And who is equal to such a task?" - 2 Corinthians 2:16.*

Your purpose and ministry are not achievable in your own strength, especially not the kind of results the Lord has in mind. You can only produce fruit and results in partnership with God. It is not only His work, for you are His vehicle, arms and legs on earth. Yet in your own strength, you will produce only paltry results. **Are you overwhelmed**

**by your tasks at hand, not knowing how to cooperate with God's purpose and grace? Are you partnering with God's grace to obtain supernatural results?** Read 2 Corinthians 6:1-2 and see that you are a co-worker with God in the purpose process.

## September 23: Abundance

*"And when I broke the seven loaves for the four thousand, how many basketfuls of pieces did you pick up?" - Mark 8:20.*

Jesus was asking this question to remind the disciples of His ability to provide not just enough but more than enough. They had an abundance when He multiplied the loaves and fish and He was using that instance to encourage them to trust Him for ongoing provision. Perhaps it is time that you also remember how well the Lord has provided for you over the years so you won't fret now over a seeming lack. When you need it, God will provide it, so if you don't have it, you must not need it—or God is teaching you another lesson about your need to trust Him. **Are you in a panic now over your finances or future? Have you ever lacked? When has God ever let you down where provision is concerned?** If you lacked, what valuable lesson did you learn? Reflect on Psalm 36 and see if it is the truth where God's abundant provision for you is concerned.

## September 24: Other Gods

*"What god is as great as our God?" - Psalm 77:13.*

There are other "gods" besides the one true God, but they are the result of human invention and demonic influence. Yet men and women serve these gods every day with their strength, time and money, and then wonder why their lives are a ruined mess. You have been spared this waste when you came to know and worship the Lord Himself. **Are you grateful for what God has done in your life? Do you take time every day to thank Him for the specific things He has done and for who He is?** Read Psalm 135 to learn the effects of worshipping false gods and then proclaim God's goodness in your own words, just like the psalmist did.

## September 25: Proficient

*"But since you do not believe what he wrote, how are you going to believe what I say?" - John 5:47.*

The Old Testament can be difficult to understand, but now that Jesus has come, we can look back and make sense of it, for most of it was describing or pointing to Jesus, His coming and His mission. When you approach it with that in mind, it becomes much easier to comprehend. **How much time do you spend studying the Old Testament? If you do, do you study it as an aide to understand what Jesus said or did?** Read John 5:39-40 and determine to be as proficient with the Old Testament as hopefully you are with the New.

## September 26: Evangelism

*"Do you think they were more guilty than all the others living in Jerusalem?" - Luke 13:4.*

When bad things happen to some, it is easy to assume that they were greater sinners than those not involved. Jesus was responding to a question about a tower falling and killing 18 people, and told those who asked to be careful for, if they did not repent, they would all likewise perish with no hope for eternity. That is quite a statement to make to religious Jews who carefully obeyed the Law! **What is your perspective on eternity? Do you see the desperate need for men and women to turn to Christ? If so, what you are doing to evangelize or support those who are?** Read Revelation 7:9- 10 and remember that salvation is not based on man's sincerity or behavior, but rather on the name and blood of Jesus.

## September 27: Denial

*"How can you say to your brother, 'Let me take the*

*speck out of your eye,' when all the time there is a plank in your own eye?" - Matthew 7:4.*

If you desire to help others, you must develop yourself to be the best you can be in the area you wish to offer help. That means you must be self-aware—knowing what you are sensing and feeling and not denying the reality in your heart. Then you can empathize and counsel those who need assistance. **Are you in denial of the reality in your heart? Do you recognize and deal with fear and other emotions?** As an example look at Peter's claim of loyalty in Matthew 26:31-35 and the painful results of that in Matthew 26:69-75.

## September 28: Benefits

*"What did you go out to see?" - Matthew 11:8.*

You put your time and energy into what you value. The people flocked to see John the Baptist, and Jesus was asking them why they went out to see John, wondering what they were looking for. **What do you go out to see? A movie? The mountains? The beach? In other words, where are you investing your time?** If Jesus is your passion and focus, then you should invest some time in learning more about Him and the ways of God. Read Mark 10:29-31 and see the benefits when you abandon casual interests for the Lord's.

## September 29: Seasons

*"How can the guests of the bridegroom mourn while he is with them?" - Matthew 9:15.*

There are seasons when certain things were appropriate and then not, but legalistic rule-makers don't want to pay attention to that. Here the Pharisees were asking Jesus why His disciples were not fasting. Jesus simply said they were busy with other things, but that eventually they would fast. **Do you prefer rules or can you be flexible where seasons of prayer, fasting and other spiritual disciplines are concerned? Do you know what time it is for you?** Read and reflect on Ecclesiastes 3:1-8 and then determine what season you are in and what the appropriate action should be on your part.

## September 30: A Lament

*"How long will the wicked be jubilant?" - Psalm 94:3.*

One of the recurring themes or questions in Psalms is why the wicked prosper while the righteous suffer. Yet every time the psalmist took up this lament, he eventually came to realize that the wicked will come to a sad end, while the righteous will enjoy their relationship with the Lord for eternity. **Have you been asking the same question or wrestling with the same paradox? Are you lamenting your own hardships when compared to the comfort of the wicked? Have you questioned the fairness of your circumstances when compared to those of another?** Read Psalm 94 in its entirety and see how the writer moved from despair to confidence, then make the same journey yourself if you have the need.

# What Would Jesus Ask You Today?

# October

## October 1: Missions

*"Am I leading a rebellion, that you have come with swords and clubs?" - Luke 22:52.*

In some parts of the world, governments oppose believers and the church with laws and even armed force. In a manner of speaking, they perceive Jesus as leading a rebellion, for His presence will overthrow wickedness and selfish special interests. This is why missions work is important, so that emissaries of the Light can confront forces of darkness. **What are you doing to support missions work? What more can you do to strengthen the persecuted church around the world?** Read Romans 15:31-32 and apply this prayer to modern missionaries so that you can undergird them in prayer.

## October 2: The Source

*"What is written in the Law?" - Luke 10:26.*

When Jesus was asked a question or challenged on what He taught concerning a particular behavior or statement, He always resorted to "the Law," which is just another term for the Word. When you think of it, Jesus only had the Old Testament, yet He was able to address all the issues of life and worship with just those Scriptures. **How much more should we be able to address our problems and establish our worldview since we have both the Old and New Testaments? Is the Word your guidebook for life's decisions? Are you growing in your ability to apply the Word as Jesus did? How can you continue to grow in that capacity?** Is Proverbs 6:20-23 your philosophy for life? If not, consider making it so.

## October 3: Hope Regained

*"My God, my God, why have you forsaken me?" - Mark 15:34.*

This question poses a problem for some, for it seems like the When

Jesus uttered these words on the cross, it sounded like the Father had abandoned Him. In a sense, He had, for Jesus bore the penalty that was due for our sins: "God made him who had no sin to be sin for us, so that in him we might become the righteousness of God" (2 Corinthians 5:21). Today's question is the first line of Psalm 22, which starts with a sound of despair but ends with a declaration of faith in God's vindication. Any Jew listening to Jesus would have known it was not a statement of anguish but of hope and trust. **Have you lost hope in some situation? Does it seem like God has abandoned you?** Then pour your heart out to Him and watch your attitude turn from dejection to hope in due time.

## October 4: Jonah's Anger

*"And should I not have concern for the great city of Nineveh . . . ?" - Jonah 4:11.*

Jonah was angry with the city of Nineveh and could not extend mercy and grace toward its inhabitants without God pressuring him to do so. The prophet was misrepresenting God, for God was not angry but the prophet was. **Are you angry with some nation, ethnic group or subgroup of the world's population, like Muslims, atheists or those with an unbiblical sexual orientation? Is it preventing you from extending or exhibiting God's love toward them? Can you put your personal preferences aside and mirror God's mercy?** Read Jonah 4 and determine if you have Jonah's anger toward anyone; then ask the Lord to soften your heart.

## October 5: Opposition

*"What is your name?" - Luke 8:30.*

Jesus asked a demon that He was confronting for its name. He wanted to know what He was dealing with, or probably more accurately wanted His disciples to know. There are some situations in which your opposition is spiritual, and it would be good to know exactly who your opponent is so you can pray accurately. **Is there**

**some situation that harasses you and represents less than God's best? Have you been focusing on the circumstances and the personalities, and not the underlying spiritual motivations?** If so, then it's time to read 2 Corinthians 10:1-6 and ask the Lord to show you the name of the spiritual opponent(s) you are facing.

## October 6: From Him

*"And if you did receive it, why do you boast as though you did not?" - 1 Corinthians 4:7.*

Whatever you have spiritually or physically, you have because of God's grace in giving it to you. You may have cooperated with the process and worked hard, but there is no cause to boast or brag, for God is still the ultimate source of all good things, including yours. **Are you proud of your looks, money, spiritual gifts or position? Are you mindful that what you have is from Him?** Read James 1:16-18 and then humble yourself and stifle your pride concerning whatever you have and whatever you have accomplished.

## October 7: Reminder

*"Have you completely forgotten this word of encouragement that addresses you as a father addresses his son?" - Hebrews 12:5.*

It is easy to forget the promises of God or the word of the Lord in the midst of life's pressures and busy-ness. That is the reason you must continually study His word and fellowship with His people in the church. Another useful discipline is to journal what the Lord has said or shown you so you can review and remember. **Are you in need of a refresher or reminder of God's promises? Do you need to pay more careful attention? Perhaps you need some time away to get refocused or re-fired up?** Read 2 Peter 3 and notice the reminders that Peter provided to the reader, just in case they forgot what they had been taught earlier. See what lessons you can learn from that chapter to help you guard against your own tendency to forget.

# October 8: Inner Talk

*"Why so disturbed within me?" - Psalm 42:11.*

It is easy to let events of the day upset you. Notice that the psalmist intiated a conversation with himself and talked himself out of being upset! It is important that you control your inner talk or it will control you! **Are your emotions out of control or at least on overload? What is the "talk" like in your mind? Is it helping or hurting your situation and peace?** Read the rest of Psalm 43:5 to see how the psalmist answered the question and then employ the same technique in your life around your area of emotional turmoil.

# October 9: Naked

*"Who told you that you were naked?" - Genesis 3:11.*

When Adam and Eve sinned, they were overcome with shame and guilt, which caused them to hide in the bush and sew fig leaves to cover their nakedness. We have been doing the same thing ever since, trying to cover ourselves in God's sight. **Are you ashamed of who you are, of your creativity, tendencies, or even your looks? What attempts have you made to 'cover' yourself? Are you actually pretending to be someone you are not? Are you afraid of failure, success, criticism, poverty, ridicule, rejection, mistakes, or anything else you consider negative?** Read and reflect on the truth in Psalm 139:13-18 and 2 Timothy 1:6-7 and then determine not to hide who you are any longer or not to be afraid to express your gifts, purpose, or creativity.

# October 10: Blame Game

*"What is this you have done?" - Genesis 3:13.*

The Lord asked Eve to explain what she had done, and she blamed her sin on the serpent but only after Adam had blamed her. They were playing the original version of the blame game in response to the wrongs they had committed. The problem is that you cannot get forgiveness and move on until you admit your sins and shortcomings instead of blaming them on your circumstances or others. **Do you take personal responsibility for your mistakes and problems and then acknowledge them to others? If you are a leader, do you take your share of blame and also share the credit?** Look at David's response to Nathan the prophet in 2 Samuel 12:1-13 when confronted with his sin, and you will see a perfect example of how to assume accountability for your actions.

## October 11: Run to Him

*"How can I give you up, Ephraim?" - Hosea 11:8.*

God's patience is magnificent! He is not only the God of a second chance, He is the God of many chances. That does not mean you should take advantage of this and test His patience, but you can count on His grace and mercy in time of need. Someone once said that when you mess up, it's time to run to God and not from Him. **Are you running to God with your failures? Or are you shrinking back, hoping to do better before you approach Him?** Read Leviticus 20:40-42 and notice how forgiving God is if anyone repents and turns to Him. How much more in Christ does the same hold true?

## October 12: Your Best

*"When you offer blind animals for sacrifice, is that not wrong?" - Malachi 1:8.*

God deserves the best that you have to offer, not the leftovers. This doesn't pertain to just church work, but to relationships, job and studies. If you focus on your circumstances, like your teachers, supervisor or pay, you may hold back, offering a lame sacrifice to the Lord. If you focus on God's goodness and your obligation to serve Him, then you will tend to give your best in every situation. **Are you giving your best to the work the Lord has for you? Has your attitude slipped and have you disengaged from those around you?**

Read Ecclesiastes 9:10, and then set a goal to do your best in every situation from this day forward.

## October 13: The Poor

*"Or do you despise the church of God and humiliate those who have nothing?" - 1 Corinthians 11:22.*

Paul continued the teaching of the Old Testament that required believers to be sensitive to the needs of the poor. You can do this not only by giving money, but also by giving yourself through volunteering or simply by willing to be close to the plight of the poor to better understand their needs and the causes of poverty. **What are you doing to help the poor? Do you know any poor folk? Are you going beyond your own culture to help the poor in other groups and nations?** Read Proverbs 19:17, and then do what you can to attract the Lord's attention in this matter as the verse promises.

## October 14: More Glorious

*"Will not the ministry of the Spirit be even more glorious?" - 2 Corinthians 3:8.*

The New Testament era is a ministry of the Spirit and it far surpasses the ministry of the Old Testament, which was one of the Law. Yet you can at times crave the structure of the Old instead of the Spirit-led lifestyle of the New. Why is that? It is because the Old provides rules to follow and obey which produces the assurance that "If I do this, then God will do that." There is no need to seek the Lord for your behavior or actions in specific situations; you just follow the Law and you are assured you have done what God wants. That is often referred to as legalism. Read Romans 8:1-17 and then ask yourself: **Am I living by the Spirit or by the flesh? Has the Spirit set me free or am I still under the bondage of the Law? Why am I more comfortable following the rules than seeking the Spirit?** Don't be in a hurry to answer but reflect on the questions to make sure you are living to the fullest in the more glorious world of God's Spirit.

# October 15: Repayment

*"How can I repay the Lord for all his goodness to me?"*
*- Psalm 116:12.*

There is nothing you can do for God that will equal what He has done for you. You can repay Him in a sense, however, by performing His will to the best of your ability as He provides the opportunities and strength! That means you will serve Him by serving His creation and people, even some who may not know Him. **Where and whom are you serving? Are you using your gifts to the fullest extent? Are you developing your potential through study and learning experiences?** Read Isaiah 6:5-8 and see how God "healed" Isaiah, and how Isaiah repaid Him by volunteering to be the Lord's spokesman.

# October 16: Lifestyle

*"Are not even the tax collectors doing that?"*
*- Matthew 5:46.*

Jesus expects that your righteous deeds will exceed those performed by those who don't know Him. While your deeds can never save you, they provide abundant evidence to those around you that you belong to Him and that He is working in your life. **Does your lifestyle differ from the world's standard to let people know you belong to God? What deeds are you performing that are above and beyond the expectations the world has for good deeds?** Read Matthew 6:1-5, and be reminded you do not do your good deeds to be seen but, when you are seen, it will be a great testimony of God's grace in your life.

# October 17: Purpose

*"But what about you?" - Mark 8:29.*

You cannot live off another person's faith or calling. Eventually, you will be required to make your own decisions about how you will live and what you will do to express your God-given purpose. **What were you created to do? What spiritual gifts do you have? What price are you willing to pay to become the best 'you' that you can be in the purpose of God?** Read Paul's instructions to Timothy in 2 Timothy 3:10-15 and then do your best to maintain the life philosophy Paul described where your own calling and purpose are concerned.

## October 18: God's Goodness

*"Why do you call me good?" - Luke 18:19.*

There are many reasons to call God good, but sometimes your perspective of His goodness can be distorted as your enemy blames God for your problems and trials. Perhaps it would be a good exercise to reflect and meditate today on why you call God good. **What has He done in your life to merit that description? What is it in His character that manifests His goodness? Have you allowed your circumstances to call God's goodness into question?** Read Job 42:1-6 and see how Job responded after his brief episode with calling into question God's motives and goodness.

## October 19: The New

*"How long will you who are simple /*
*love your simple ways?" - Proverbs 1:22.*

You cannot keep doing the same things and expect different results. To get new or better results, you must step out of your ruts and comfort zones and not make excuses for why you are not more productive or fruitful. **Where have you stopped developing or trying to grow? Where do you have wishful thinking, hoping for something new while you cling to old habits and practices?** Read Matthew 9:17 and see that you must change your wineskin before you put in new wine. **Where in life are you in need of those new wineskins?**

# October 20: Dullness

*"Are you so dull?" - Mark 7:18.*

The disciples could not comprehend what Jesus was talking about and he called them "dull." He was not trying to be offensive, but rather describing their spiritual condition. You must work to sharpen your spiritual senses so that you can discern and analyze things from a spiritual perspective. That requires both desire and effort. **Are you spiritually astute? Have you worked to put off spiritual dullness and made the effort to grow spiritually? How can you increase that effort to become even more spiritually intelligent?** Read the process Paul described in Ephesians 4:17-24, and then apply those steps to your life over and over again.

# October 21: Surprise

*"Men of Israel, why does this surprise you?" - Acts 3:12.*

God is a God of surprises, for He does not act or think like we do. Most of the surprises come when we trust Him for some outcome, but have no idea how He will bring it about—but He does in His own unique manner. Sometimes He surprises us when we expect Him to act in judgment and He acts in grace. At other times, He bestows on us insight or revelation into His word that specifically addresses a need we have. And finally, it is always a surprise as to how much God loves us. **When is the last time you were surprised in your walk with the Lord? How long ago was it when you trusted Him for that which you could not anticipate or expect? Have you cooperated lately with the Lord to produce a surprise blessing the life of someone else?** Read the verses preceding today's question in Acts 3:1-11 and then determine to help produce or see the kind of surprise contained in that story.

# October 22: Inner Peace

*"Why so disturbed within me?" - Psalm 43:5.*

It is a sign of maturity that you can manage and even control your inner man with the help of the Spirit—that is, if you want that kind of help. There may even be times when you need to seek some counselors to help you out with your emotions and thought life. **Do anger, fear, bitterness or worry overwhelm you? Do you live in a state of peace or a state of anxiety and being upset?** As a superb example of this, read Acts 16:22-28 and see how Paul and Silas were at peace even after they had been abused and beaten. then determine to find this same peace and self-control in your own anxious moments.

## October 23: The Climb

*"Who may ascend the mountain of the Lord?"*
*- Psalm 24:3.*

It is a privilege to ascend to the heights God has assigned to you, but it also requires hard work and effort on your part. God will not pick you up and carry you there, but He will empower and energize you to complete the climb and enjoy the fruit of your labors. Once you arrive, you will also have a spectacular view of God's purpose. **Are you exerting enough effort to complete your climb? Are you enjoying the journey? Are you relishing the view of climbing higher into God's purpose?** Read Ecclesiastes 2:24-26, and ask yourself if you are enjoying your work or simply climbing your mountain for someone else's benefit.

## October 24: Failure

*"Do you truly love me more than these?" - John 21:15.*

Jesus posed this question to Peter three times after Peter had denied the Lord three times, knowing that Peter had to face his failure in order to move on. Once Peter affirmed his love for Jesus, Jesus reiterated Peter's mission by telling him to "feed my lambs." **Are you grappling with some failure in your life?** The way forward is not to ignore it. Instead, you must face it for what it is, learn from it, and then refocus on fulfilling your purpose from that point forward, acknowledging God's magnificent grace allowing you to do so. Read how Samson recovered from his failures to ultimately succeed in Judges 16:23-31, and then work to do the same as you bounce back from yours.

## October 25: Remember

*"Don't you remember that when I was with you I used to tell you these things?" - 2 Thessalonians 1:5.*

Paul was reminding the disciples of his teaching while he had been with them. Jesus taught and four gospel writers recorded what He said so you and I can remember and reflect. **How do you help remember the important things you have been taught, things that someone paid a price to give you? What price are you paying to deliver the truth God has given you to others so they can read, hear and remember? Do you write? Journal? Record and disseminate? Study?** Read 2 Peter 1:12-15, and notice what Peter did and why he did it, and then take steps to make sure you remember and help others remember what God has done in and through you.

## October 26: Learning Curve

*"Why do you try to test God by putting on the necks of the disciples a yoke that neither we nor our fathers have been able to bear?" - Acts 15:10.*

There was probably a day when you did not know right from wrong, and you were estranged from the Lord. Then you came to know Him, but you still had a steep learning curve of what it meant to serve and please the Lord. God was gracious to you during those times. **Are you gracious to those who are where you were before or right after you met the Lord? Do you expect more from them than they can possibly produce? Have you forgotten where you came from and how far you have come?** Read 1 Corinthians 13 and then ask God to develop in you the love described there for all people, but especially for the lost and newly found.

# October 27: Projection

*"So when you, a mere man, pass judgment on them and yet do the same things, do you think you will escape God's judgment?" - Romans 2:3.*

It is easy to look at someone and be disgusted by their attitude or behavior, yet have the same problem present in your own life. It's called projection and, in some sense, you are causing others to carry the pain of your own failure and sin. Rather than judge it in yourself, you judge it in others. And you can be hardest on those who happen to have the same faults as you. **Are you judgmental toward someone while you carry the same problem? Do you act self-righteously toward those who are proud, yet have pride in your own life?** Follow the procedure Jesus described in Matthew 7:1-5 and you will not fall into this common tendency.

# October 28: Relationships

*"For what do righteousness and wickedness have in common?" - 2 Corinthians 6:14.*

Of course, the answer to today's question is they have nothing in common, for they are as incompatible as light and darkness. What's more, one is superior to the other, just like light is to darkness. This question is posed in the context of Paul's teaching that a believer should not be unequally yoked with an unbeliever except for certain circumstances. In other words, in most cases it's not wise to join forces with someone who does not know the Lord, especially in business or marriage. **Are you suffering due to some relationship with an unbeliever? Has their idolatry or values system rubbed off on you? What can you do you do going forward to be free of these ties? If nothing, then how can you reinforce yourself spiritually to continue to grow and obey the Lord?** Read the context of the question in 2 Corinthians 6:14-18 and then, if possible, divest yourself of all inappropriate relationships as quickly as you can.

# October 29: The Depths

*"How is it that they say the Christ is the Son of David?"*
*- Luke 20:40.*

You will only plumb the depths of Scripture's wisdom and insight if you challenge yourself to pose and answer good questions. In this case, Jesus asked His opponents about how the Old Testament could label the Messiah to also be a Son of David. This indicated that the Messiah was not only of the tribe of Judah, but also that He was a human and not exclusively a divine being. **What questions are you pondering where the Scriptures are concerned?** This was Jesus' style of teaching and learning even when He was twelve years old, as you can see in Luke 2:46-52. Perhaps it should be your style, too?

# October 30: Judges

*"Do you not know that the saints will judge the world?"*
*- 1 Corinthians 6:2.*

Many are infatuated with end time fantasies, but the end is not only about His return. It's also about the role the saints will have once the new heaven and new earth are formed. As part of that new era, the saints will judge the world! Those who have been judged by the world system will then take their turn to evaluate the world according to God's standards. **Are you getting ready for this role? Are you reading, learning and growing to gain wisdom and sharpen your discernment?** When you read 1 Corinthians 4:4-5, you get the sense that God will guide this process but that you will be involved as co-judges. Get ready!

# October 31: God's Name in Vain

*"How long will you people turn my glory into shame?"*
*- Psalm 4:2.*

You have a relationship with the God of the universe. He has promised to be with you to the ends of the earth, to hear and answer your prayers, to empower you to meet every trial and challenge, and to fight your battles and overcome your enemies. **With all this potential and power, what are you accomplishing for and through Him? What are you doing as His representative to further His kingdom? What great thing are you striving to do with His help?** Read Exodus 20:7 and consider whether this refers to using God's name as a curse word or if it really refers to having the name of the Lord to use in prayer and action and not doing anything with it!

# What Would Jesus Ask You Today?

# November

## November 1: New Rules

*"Why, as though you still belonged to it [the world], do you submit to its rules?" - Colossians 2:20.*

You have died to the world and are alive in Christ, set free to serve Him and His purpose. Yet your flesh is holding out, rebelling against the new rules of God's kingdom. That is why you are still tempted to follow the world and its ways, even though you belong to Jesus. **Are you walking in the power of your new life? Are you still following the rules of the world system instead of a lifestyle of faith?** Read Romans 6 and seek God's help and power to walk out these new rules in the new life you have found in Christ.

## November 2: Your Body

*"Do you not know that your bodies are members of Christ himself?" - 1 Corinthians 6:15.*

Paul posed this question in the context of sexual purity and ethics. Your body is not your own; it belongs to Jesus by nature of the fact that you died and were raised into Him. Therefore you are not free to make decisions about how to use your body; you must consider and follow His will. **Are you following Jesus' commands where sex is concerned? Are you behaving like you belong to Him?** Read Genesis 2:21-25 and see where God's plan for marriage and sex began; His plans haven't changed since then.

## November 3: Persecution

*"Why then do you accuse me of blasphemy because I said, 'I am God's Son'?" - John 10:36.*

It is sometimes hard to believe that people persecuted Jesus, but they did. Jesus had no sin, went about doing good, spoke with authority and taught with creative excellence, and still sinful men spoke evil against Him and eventually crucified Him. **Can you expect any less?**

**Are you experiencing persecution for His name's sake? For your stand as a believer?** If you are, then rejoice and be glad, just like the apostles did in Acts 4:27-42.

## November 4: Negative Thoughts

*"Why, my soul, are you downcast?" - Psalm 42:5.*

**Do circumstances in your life have you down? Are you suffering from depression?** How you talk to yourself can affect how you feel. In other words, your thinking, which is something you can control, contributes to your emotional and mental state of being. Instead of telling yourself how bad things are, take time to recite the blessings you have. If you can't do that, then focus on God's promises in the Bible and speak them out loud if necessary. If you simply give in to your negative thoughts, however, then you will indeed be downcast. Read Mark 14:32-36 and see that Jesus was downcast and what He did to combat it. Then do the same.

## November 5: Family Benefits

*"From whom do the kings of the earth collect duty and taxes—from their own sons or from others?" - Matthew 17:25.*

You are a child of God. That affords you benefits not available to those who don't know Him. What kinds of benefits? He hears and answers your prayers; He grants you health; He prospers your way; He provides for your needs; He forgives your sins. **Are you living in the fullness of these family privileges? Are you thankful for all that God is doing for you?** Read Psalm 103 and then spend the day enumerating and being grateful for being part of the family of God.

## November 6: Anguish

*"Why are you so far from saving me, so far from my cries of anguish?" - Psalm 22:1.*

Anguish is a word that describes deep emotional trauma, usually the result of some tragic event. During those times in your life, you can conclude that God doesn't listen to your cries for help because He doesn't care. Yet God is using these difficult times to shape and mold you into the image of Christ and teach you many valuable things. In those dark days, it is necessary (but difficult) to trust even more than during normal times. **Does it feel like God has abandoned you? Are you crying out yet getting no response?** Read what Jesus told His disciples about grief and joy in John 16:20-22 and then have faith that the same will be true for you, no matter how tough the times may be.

## November 7: Withholding

*"Can he supply meat for his people?" - Psalm 78:20.*

God is able to provide for all His people, but at times He withholds some of His provision to teach and test you, to see if you will trust Him and not your circumstances. **Are you going through a tough time financially? Does it seem like God is withholding what you need and you are suffering for it?** Read Deuteronomy 8:2-4 and see why the Lord may be doing this, and begin to change your focus to one of thanksgiving and praise, even in the midst of your lack.

## November 8: For You

*"For what god is there in heaven or on earth who can do the deeds and mighty works you do?" - Deuteronomy 3:24.*

You know God can do anything. **But do you believe and know that He can do anything for you?** You know God can heal. **Do you believe He will heal you?** You know God can provide miraculously. **Do you believe that He will provide miraculously for you? Are you living a lifestyle where God has to do mighty works for you to be successful?** Read Paul's prayer in Ephesians 3:14-21 and ask whether or not the power needed for God to do miraculous works resides in you. If it does, let the miracles flow!

## November 9: Greatness

*"What other nation is so great as to have such righteous decrees and laws as this body of laws I am setting before you today?" - Deuteronomy 4:8.*

You don't have to obey the Lord; you are privileged to! God declared Israel a great nation because they received His Law and not due to military or economic might. Their relationship determined their greatness in God's eyes. **Do you see yourself as great because of what God has done for you? Are you walking in the power of this by rejoicing in, studying and obeying God's word?** Psalm 19:7-11 shows there is great reward in receiving and obeying God's commands.

## November 10: The Voice of God

*"Has any other people heard the voice of God speaking out of fire, as you have, and lived?" - Deuteronomy 4:33.*

It was rare, and even somewhat dangerous, to hear the voice of God in Old Testament times. Today it is common, for heaven is always speaking "loudly" as you can see in Revelation. God speaks through circumstances, His Word, other people (even some who don't know Him), and in a still, small voice. **Are you heeding the voice of God? What is He saying to you these days? What is His theme for your life?** Read Hebrews 12:18-29, and be diligent to hear, remember and obey the things God is telling you.

## November 11: Gideon

*"These nations are stronger than we are. How can we drive them out?" - Deuteronomy 7:17.*

Perhaps you are facing overwhelming circumstances that you don't see how you will ever overcome. Maybe it is some nagging, ongoing heart sin. It could also be some external issue, like financial lack or someone you love who is not doing well. Israel asked today's question because they saw their opposition as more powerful than God, with them them powerless to address that disparity. Is that your perspective? Do you know God can do anything, but you aren't sure if He can or will do anything for you in your current state? Are you stuck in bitterness or discouragement? Read the beginning of Gideon's story in Judges 6:11-16 and see if you are responding to God as Gideon did, with complaints and an angry or unbelieving heart.

## November 12: All In

*"What does the Lord your God ask of you but . . . to love him, to serve the Lord your God with all your heart and with all your soul, . . . ?" - Deuteronomy 10:12.*

God does not require casual followers, but those who are completely sold out to Him, His purpose and His will. He is not looking for people who go to church and then proceeds to live their lives according to their own desires. **Are you "all in" where the Lord is concerned? Have you committed your finances, future and relationships to Him and His will? What evidence is there that you are all in?** Read the story of Zacchaeus in Luke 19:1-10 and see how he abandoned his career and money to the Lord and follow His example.

## November 13: Attitude

*"What do you see?" - Zechariah 4:2.*

"What do you see?" - Zechariah 4:2.
God is always bringing things into and through your life. How you see them determines your attitude and behavior toward them. If you frame them as problems, you may respond with anger and frustration, and be stressed out. If you see them as opportunities for growth and learning more about Him, you may respond with enthusiasm and creativity. Either way, your attitude is always a choice. **What do**

**you see in your life right now? Do you see lack or abundance? Pain or joy? Opportunities or problems?** Read 1 Samuel 17 and see how Israel saw Goliath as someone too big to hit, and thus they retreated, but David saw someone too big to miss, so he fought. In both cases, it was their attitude that determined how they would respond, and their attitude was shaped by their assumptions and perspective.

## November 14: Worthless

*"It may seem marvelous to the remnant of this people at that time, but will it seem marvelous to me?" - Zechariah 8:6.*

The Lord is not always impressed with the things man holds in high regard. The world honors strong, bold leaders, while the Lord honors humble ones. The world is impressed by those who build tall buildings or mighty kingdoms. The Lord is impressed by those who build His Church. **Are you involved in things that are marvelous to the world system or in the eyes of God? To what are you devoting the best of your energy, talents and gifts? Where are you investing your money?** Read Acts 12:21-24 for an example of something the people honored as great but God regarded as worthless.

## November 15: Your Best

*"When you sacrifice lame or diseased animals, is that not wrong?" - Malachi 1:8.*

Old Testament sacrifices were made to gain God's favor and approval. That is no longer necessary because Jesus paid the price for you to have a relationship with the Lord. You should, however, still offer God your best as a token of thanks and worship, not as an act to gain approval. **Are you giving God and His people your best? Are you doing things, whether in church or out, beyond the norm or acceptable standard as an act of devotion?** Read Malachi 1:12-14 and apply the principles from that directive to your walk with the Lord.

## November 16: Wisdom

*"You fools, when will you become wise?" - Psalm 94:8.*

You do not obtain wisdom except through hard work. First get knowledge and then discover how to apply it to everyday life. Proverbs informs you that you get wisdom by asking for it, by paying attention to God's answers to your seeking, by studying Proverbs, and by walking with the wise in a mentoring or learning relationship. **Are you wise? Are you diligently working toward that goal? Do people seek you out for wisdom? What are you doing to increase your wisdom?** Read Proverbs 1:1-2, 2:2-5, 8:1 and 13:20, and set a course that will enable you to obtain and increase wisdom.

## November 17: He Hears

*"Does he who fashioned the ear not hear?" - Psalms 94:9.*

God made your ear to hear, so He certainly understands hearing. What's more, He Himself hears and perfectly understands exactly what you mean! That means God hears your prayers, even the thoughts of your heart. **If that's true, why don't you pray more? Why don't you talk to Him more during your day? Since He knows your heart, why hesitate to verbalize what you think, since He already knows?** Read 1 Thessalonians 5:16-18 and spend some time talking to God today, the One who is the perfect listener.

## November 18: God is Watching

*"Does he who formed the eye not see?" - Psalm 94:9.*

The Lord not only sees your predicament, He also sees your actions along with those of your enemies. You cannot hide from Him and just because He does not react, does not mean He doesn't see or that He approves. He also may not reward you for your good deeds, but that again does not mean He has not seen and is pleased. God has a big book and a sharp pencil, so to speak, and records all you do for and to His people, for good and not so good. **Are you behaving like God is watching and recording your every act, regardless of whether or not the consequences are immediate? Are you laying up treasure in heaven by doing good deeds, regardless if others notice? Are you 'cutting corners' on excellence, figuring that no one is paying attention—forgetting that God is?** Read Esther 6 and notice how the king honored Mordecai for his faithfulness after a long delay; then picture the Lord doing the same thing for you in due time.

## November 19: The Nations

*"Does he who disciplines nations not punish?"*
*- Psalms 94:10.*

God is so powerful that He can order history and events not only to punish individuals but also entire nations! That is why the work of missions and outreach is so important, for God is weighing nations and is ready to punish those who are found lacking, including Muslim, Communist, Hindu and capitalist states. **Do you believe that God requires obedience of all nations and will judge those who disobey? Do you believe that Jesus is the focal point of this obedience and the only means by which people have access to God?** Read 1 John 5:11-12, and see that Jesus is the only source of life. That means anyone not in Him already resides in death.

## November 20: Creativity

*"Does he who teaches mankind lack knowledge?"*
*- Psalm 94:10.*

George Washington Carver discovered more than 300 uses for the peanut and 100 uses for the sweet potato. What was the secret of his creativity? He prayed and asked God to show him the secrets of the peanut and potato. God still has knowledge that will help mankind and yes, even you, to creatively unlock and harnass the secrets of His creation. **Do you have any ideas for an invention or innovation?**

**Do you have a burden to solve some problem that you and others are facing? Do you have a desire to beautify your part of the world with some creative expression that will inspire and uplift others?** Read Exodus 31:1-11 and then ask God for some of His knowledge and wisdom that will enable you to create something like Bezalel did in the power of God's Spirit. Once you pray, then summon the courage to pursue your creative dream.

## November 21: One Standard

*"Can a corrupt throne be allied with you—a throne that brings on misery by its decrees?" - Psalm 94:20.*

God holds all nations and leaders responsible for integrity and righteousness, whether they acknowledge Him or not. You may be leading your garden club or your company, but that is no different than if you were leading your church. God's standards are to be honored and observed no matter what you are doing. **Do you treat your current work and position as if it was your ministry? Do you treat all people fairly and judge with fairness?** Read Obadiah 1:15-18 and see how the Lord spoke to those nations just like He did to Israel. Understand that the Lord has one standard for all people.

## November 22: God Sings

*"Who will bring any charge against those whom God has chosen?" - Romans 8:33.*

Of course, no one should bring a charge but your enemy Satan and his workers are constantly accusing you before God and His people. You can overcome his tactics by walking in the truth that God does not condemn or accuse; to the contrary, God loves and rejoices over you! **Does an inner voice or thought condemn you for your weaknesses or failures? Do you wallow in guilt when you fail?** If so, read Zephaniah 3:9-17 and enter into the truth in that passage that God is rejoicing and singing over you.

## November 23: Free Will

*"What do you prefer?" - 1 Corinthians 4:21.*

Many are comfortable in a perpetual state of servant-hood, willing to do whatever the Lord asks. At some point, God wants to see what is in your heart to do that is based on His word shaping your will. In the short letter to Philemon, Paul indicated that he could order Philemon to do something, but he preferred that Philemon carry it out of his own free will. **What is in your heart to do? Why aren't you doing it? What are you waiting for?** First take a look at Paul's words to Philemon in 8-9 and 14; then go do the good deeds that are in your heart without waiting on confirmation or heavenly direction.

## November 24: Identify with Others

*"Who is weak, and I do not feel weak?"*
*- 2 Corinthians 11:29.*

Paul set a high standard for love of others and modeled it in his pastoral ministry. He urged all disciples to so identify with others that they would feel what others felt. That requires that the disciples like you be close to one another, know what the others are going through and work to empathize and identify with the status and pain of others. **Are you this close to other believers? Do you identify so keenly with them that you feel their pain or joy?** This can only happen through God's love working in you as Paul and the apostles emphasized again and again as seen in 2 John 1:1-6. Do you have that kind of love working in you?

## November 25: Loyalty

*"Do two walk together unless they have agreed to do so?" - Amos 3:3.*

Loyalty is a godly trait that enables you to commit to someone else despite their and your imperfections. It requires patience, forgiveness, commitment, and abandoning the right to quit. Of course, your ultimate loyalty is to God, but He can bring other relationships into your life and require that you express loyalty to Him though them. That means their problems become yours, their happiness is your goal, and their best interests are paramount. **Are you a loyal person? Is your loyalty ultimately to God, or is it to doctrine, politics, or your own needs?** There are many examples of loyalty in the Bible, but perhaps the most moving is Ruth. Read about her in Ruth 1:6-18 and then seek to follow her example of loyalty and commitment to the situation God has placed you in these days. Then read Galatians 5:13-15 for some practical advice on how to walk with others.

## November 26: Encourage Yourself

*"Why, my soul, are you downcast" - Psalm 43:5.*

It is easy to get down and discouraged when things do not go well or when nothing happens at all! You can lose sight of the Lord and what He is doing in and around you. It is then that you have to encourage yourself, since no one else is going to do it for you. **Are you downcast? Are things not going as you think or wish they should? Are you tired of living like that?** Then it's time to take charge of your encouragement! Read Jude 1:24-25, and encourage yourself in your battle with discouragement and maybe even depression.

## November 27: A Rational Decision

*"In God I trust and am not afraid.*
*What can man do to me?" - Psalm 56:11.*

Man can reject, ridicule, torture and even take your life. Yet if your life is in Him, they cannot take it. They can only transfer it from one realm to another, which Jesus alluded to in Luke 12:5. All things considered, therefore, men cannot do much to you if you are in Him. The psalmist came to that conclusion and boldly declared his trust in the Lord and his decision not to be afraid. **Why not follow the**

**psalmist's example and make a calculated, rational decision to trust Him with your life and future and not be afraid?** When David was faced with a terrible and dangerous situation, he encouraged himself in the Lord and prayed as described in 1 Samuel 30:1-8. Perhaps you should learn to do the same?

## November 28: Grow Up

*"Who is wise? Let them realize these things. Who is discerning?" - Hosea 14:9.*

God expects you to grow in your ability to discern, understand and apply spiritual things. What's more, you are not only to grow in them personally, but also be available to help others grow as well. In other words, God wants you to grow up and be a source of wisdom for others because of your victorious lifestyle as an overcomer. **Are you growing in the things of the Lord? Are you a source of wisdom and insight for others?** Read Ezra 9:1-6 and see how Ezra's wisdom impacted those around him, and how the whole nation exhibited wisdom and discernment as they repented and prayed.

## November 29: Worship Now

*"Who is this that appears like the dawn, fair as the moon, bright as the sun, majestic as the stars in procession?" - Song of Solomon 6:10.*

It is impossible to describe the Lord's beauty or majesty, but that does not prevent you from trying. That is what is called worship, when you talk or sing about the Lord and His attributes. This is not for God's benefit, for He certainly knows who He is. Rather it is for your benefit, so you can keep your focus on the Magnificent One while you encounter the trials and uncertainties of life. **Are you a person given to extravagant worship? Do you find it easy to express your love and adoration for the Lord of lords?** Read Revelation 7:7-17, and realize that this picture of worship may not just be for heaven, but also for the church as it worships Him now.

# November 30: Only You

*"Who shall separate us from the love of Christ?"*
*- Romans 8:35.*

No one can separate you from the love of Christ and its effects, unless you allow them to do so. That in some sense means that you are the only one who can separate you from God's love! **Are you allowing someone else to rob you of the joy you have in Christ? Are you aware that it is your decision that has allowed this to happen? So, if you decided to let that happen, why not decide not to let it happen?** Read Luke 14:25-27 to see that you cannot allow even those closest to you to come between you and Jesus.

# What Would Jesus Ask You Today?

# December

## December 1: Wisdom Calling

*"Does not understanding raise her voice?"
- Proverbs 8:1.*

According to this question, the wisdom you need is not only available, but is making itself known to you by broadcasting its presence. That means if you pay attention, you will find the answers to those tough or seemingly complex problems you are encountering. **Are you stuck in some dilemma and need advice and answers for the way out? Are you so focused on the problem that you cannot hear the solution that is calling out to you?** Read 1 Samuel 25:1-24 and see how David had made a wrong decision but wisdom showed up through Abigail to correct his steps.

## December 2: Make Time

*"Do not my words do good to the one whose ways are upright?" - Micah 2:7.*

Even though you may be busy, you need to find time for God's word, for it is the only book written thousands of years ago that can still give you guidance today and also judge the "thoughts and intentions of [your] heart" (Hebrews 4:12). It can tell you whether or not you are loving your spouse, are doing good work on the job, or have a right heart attitude toward others. **How much time are you devoting to the study of God's word these days? Why is it that you are too busy? What can you do to make the Word a priority?** Read Proverbs 4 to be reminded how important it is to pay attention to God's words and instructions.

## December 3: Your Problem

*"Do you want to get well?" - John 5:6.*

This is a curious question, for who would not want to get well? It is possible, however, to lack faith to believe you can be well. It is also possible to become emotionally attached to your problem and the attention it brings you. You can even use your problem to manipulate and control other people. **Are you emotionally attached to your problem? Has your problem become so much a part of your identity that you cannot let it go?** Read Matthew 5:29-31 and notice how ruthlessly Jesus expects you to deal with your temptations and problems.

## December 4: Minimum Requirements

*"How could one man chase a thousand, or two put ten thousand to flight, unless their Rock had sold them, unless the Lord had given them up?" - Deuteronomy 32:30.*

There is no way the enemies of God's people can overcome His people unless His people do not meet the requirements for God's protection. He can intervene in our situations and bring us great success and victory if we meet the minimum requirements. Those requirements are: 1) have faith in God that He can do it for you; 2) operate in your purpose, God's will for your life; and 3) do things God's way according to His word in order to please Him. if you don't do those things and stubbornly refuse to pursue His will, He will give you over to your enemies (things like fear, doubt, and idolatry). **So is God the Rock in your world? Do you meet those minimum requirements or are you shrinking back in fear and insecurity? Do you have victory over your enemies or do your enemies triumph over you?** Read Proverbs 16:7 and then work to make that promise a reality in your own life. If that promise is not activated in your life, ask the Rock why it is not--and then make the necessary changes.

## December 5: Touch Him

*"Do you believe I can do this?" - Matthew 9:28.*

Most people answer this question with a resounding yes. They know God is all powerful and can do anything. The real question is whether or not they believe He will do something for them now at their point of need. Then they may respond, "I'm not sure," or a straight up no. **Is there any unbelief working in your life preventing God from doing something miraculous for you or for those closest to you? What can you do to activate your faith to see God do good things for you?** Read Matthew 14:25-26 and see how the faith of those who reached out to touch Jesus' garments were healed. Then find a way to reach out and touch Him yourself.

## December 6: Shining Light

*"Is a lamp brought to be put under a basket or under a bed rather than on a lampstand?" - Mark 4:21.*

Many are ambivalent about referring to their good deeds, gifts or accomplishments. Somehow it seems self-promoting or un-Christian. **Yet how else will people know how you can help them or what God has done in your life unless you talk about how God is in your life? Do you share in this ambivalence? Do you find it difficult to refer to yourself? Or are you comfortable doing it, realizing that it glorifies what God has done in your life and may encourage and help others?** Read Matthew 5:14-16 and then let the light of your purpose and gifts shine forth for the world to see.

## December 7: Arguing

*"What were you arguing about on the road?" - Mark 9:33.*

It is easy to get into an argument, especially with fellow believers over doctrine and biblical interpretation. In this verse, Jesus asked the question because they were arguing over whose ministry was most significant. Jesus confronted them, because arguing is the opposite of how He wants His followers to behave toward one another. **Are you prone to arguing with others? Do you have to win every debate? Do you talk more than listening, avoiding grasping other's positions?** Titus 3:9-11 shows how Paul directed the church to handle someone who was argumentative and divisive.

## December 8: Offended

*"Does this offend you?" - John 6:61.*

Jesus was teaching about eating His body and blood in John 6, and many people misunderstood, were offended, scandalized and consequently withdrew from following Him. You should expect not to comprehend all that God says and does, for His ways are higher than yours. Yet things can happen that you thought God would never do, say or allow, and you can find yourself offended and disillusioned. **Are you currently questioning what God has done? Are you stumbling over what He has allowed that to you is inconsistent with love and mercy?** Read Matthew 11:6, and then do all you can to stay blessed by not stumbling over some of the more difficult things you will encounter in the Lord.

## December 9: Hypocrisy

*"Did not the one who made the outside make the inside also?" - Luke 11:40.*

The Pharisees were concerned that Jesus did not wash His hands according to their tradition, but Jesus countered with the fact that God is concerned more with man's inner life than outward appearances or conditions. Often your culture, whether societal, family, or church, can cause you to try and hide, from others and even from God, your true heart condition, and that can lead to deception and hypocrisy as you act one way for the public while your heart is in another place. **Have you become more concerned with externals than your heart? How you look than how you are? What others think more than what God thinks?** Read 1 Samuel 15:10-31 and see how Saul was more concerned with how he looked before the people than before God, which led to his eventual downfall.

## December 10: Fruitful

*"Do people pick grapes from thornbushes or*

*figs from thistles?" - Matthew 7:16.*

Jesus was talking about His expectation that lovers of God and His disciples would bear appropriate and abundant fruit in their lives. This fruit was not just to be the absence of certain destructive behaviors but the presence of constructive actions such as evangelism, compassion, patience and good deeds. **Are you bearing fruit or just staying out of trouble? Is your lack of sinful behavior because of love for God or fear of getting caught? On what area of active, tangible fruit does God want you to focus today?** Read John 15:1-8 and see that God wants so much fruit that, when you are fruitful, He will prune you to make you even more so!

## December 11: Active Faith

*"When the Son of Man comes,*
*will he find any faith on earth?" - Luke 18:8.*

Jesus was always amazed and saddened that He did not find active faith among His people. He always responded when He saw it, however, as we read in Luke 5:17-26 when He saw the faith of the men who lowered their friend through the roof for healing. **If He comes to your house looking for faith today, will He find it? What would you show Him that represents your active faith? Would He be amazed to find it or amazed that there is little to none?** Read Jesus' amazing words in John 14:12-14 and then determine whether or not you are achieving any greater works through your faith and prayers.

## December 12: Give Thanks

*"Has none but this foreigner returned to*
*give thanks to God?" - Luke 17:18.*

Jesus healed a group of lepers, but only one returned to give thanks. This impacted Jesus so deeply that He mentioned it to His disciples. Thanksgiving therefore must be important to Him. **How thankful**

**have you been lately? Do you hold what God has done for you uppermost in your mind and heart, or dwell on what you wish He would do? Does your lack affect your gratitude for what you do have?** Read Luke 17:11-19. You can almost hear the disappointment in Jesus' voice as He asks today's question.

## December 13: Edify

*"What are you discussing together as you walk along?" - Luke 24:17.*

When people are together, there are a number of things to discuss. Some of those things are uplifting, some are useless and others are downright sinful. **Are you using your connection time with other people to build them up? Are you using that time to discuss meaningful things, or to gossip, complain or be sarcastic?** Read Ephesians 5:1-4, and then determine that today you will use your mouth during your encounters with others to talk about uplifting things that will edify you and others.

## December 14: Work and Rest

*"Are there not twelve hours of daylight?" - John 11:9.*

On the equator, the days and nights are equal, which means that you should divide your time equally between work and non-work, non-rest and rest. **Do you have your daily rhythm established? Are your work or rest patterns out of whack, with either one dominating the other? Do you enjoy your work? Do you gain benefit from your rest?** Read Exodus 20:8-10, and then reflect on the importance of practicing good work and rest ethics in your walk with the Lord.

## December 15: More Stuff

*"Man, who appointed me a judge or*

*an arbiter between you?" - Luke 12:14.*

A man asked Jesus to tell his brother to split an inheritance, and Jesus posed today's question. He went on to warn the asker and crowd to guard against all kinds of greed, for life does not consist of an abundance of possessions. **Are you keeping that in mind? Do you hold a grudge or bitterness against someone because you lost some "stuff" to them? Are you trying to use Jesus to help you keep or get your "stuff"?** Read Ecclesiastes 4:6-8 and see if the vain pursuit of more "stuff" has clouded your perspective and walk with Him.

## December 16: Separated

*"Shall trouble or hardship or persecution or famine or nakedness or danger or sword?" - Romans 8:35.*

Paul was asking if any of the above-mentioned things could separate us from the love of God. The answer of course is no, except if you allow them to separate you from Him. Paul did not think it strange that those negative experiences would find their way into your life; he found it incomprehensible that they could drive a wedge between you and the Lord without your permission. **Have unexpected, difficult times separated you from God's love? Are you depressed, discouraged, or disillusioned? Can you see that it is how you have processed those things that have caused a separation between you and the Lord?** Read Job 1:18-21 and then ask God's help to replicate Job's response to the hardship that has come into his life.

## December 17: Prayer Habits

*"Couldn't you men keep watch with me for one hour?" - Matthew 26:40.*

By keeping watch, Jesus was referring to a time of prayer. The men could not do it as they were tired and sorrowful, and their humanity got the best of them (their spirits were willing, but their flesh was weak). **How is your prayer life these days? Are you watching**

**and praying for any period of time or has your human weakness overwhelmed your ability to focus? Are you disciplined in your prayer habits or are they random?** As you approach the busy holidays and a new year, read what Jesus had to say about prayer in Matthew 6:5-15 and ask His help in establishing better prayer habits

## December 18: Now and Then

*"And if you are to judge the world, are you not competent to judge trivial cases?" - 1 Corinthians 6:2.*

The next age is not one endless song service. There is purpose for you 'then' just like there is 'now.' That is why you learn and grow in the Lord 'now,' for you will retain what you know and learn 'now' to be used again 'then.' And part of your preparation for 'then' is to sharpen your discernment and gain wisdom to exercise in your family, work, and ministry right 'now.' **Are you growing in wisdom? Are you allowing the Lord to put you in tough situations so you can judge the problem and recommend a solution?** Take a look at Luke 12:56-58 and see that Jesus rebuked His followers when they did not have the wisdom to handle their own 'now' matters. He later promised they would 'then' sit on thrones and judge the twelve tribes in Matthew 19:28!

## December 19: A Promise is a Promise

*"Or do I make my plans in a worldly manner so that in the same breath I say both 'Yes, yes' and 'No, no'?" - 2 Corinthians 1:17.*

Paul said it is a worldly, ungodly habit to say you are going to do something and then not follow through with your commitment. That includes saying, "I will pray for you" and not doing so, or "I'll call you" and then failing to call. **Do you say yes and no in the same breath? Is your word your bond or do you consider it permissible not to follow through as long as you were sincere when you made the promise?** Do you believe "I forgot" is a legitimate excuse when you gave your word to do something and didn't do it? Read Joshua 9:18-20 and see that Israel could not punish its neighbors who had deceived them because Joshua had made a promise, and Israel had to keep that promise because Joshua had given his word on their behalf. That's how seriously God takes what you say and the promises and vows you make!

## December 20: Take Stock

*"What have you done?" - Genesis 4:10.*

It is always good to take stock of what you are and are not doing, repenting and making changes where necessary. For instance, ask these questions: **What have I done for the poor? Have I offended others? What have I done that has pleased the Lord? What can I do to please Him more? Are there sins I have not confessed and for which I have not asked forgiveness?** Read and pray Psalm 139:23-24 and rely on God to help you answer today's question.

## December 21: Christmas Focus

*"But who can endure the day of his coming?" - Malachi 3:2.*

If not for God's mercy, no one could endure His coming. But God did not send Jesus on a white horse or wrapped in royal robes, but sent a baby, wrapped in swaddling clothes and born to humble parents in an obscure town south of Jerusalem. And He did not send Him to judge but to save. **Do you have the proper focus for this Christmas season?** Take time today to read part of the Christmas story in Matthew 1:18-25 and meditate on God's mercy that has allowed you access to His throne of grace through Christ.

## December 22: Bow Down

*"Who can stand when he appears?" - Malachi 3:2.*

Malachi was indicating that when the servant of the Lord called

Messiah appeared, it would be an event to impact all people in all nations. All would bow to His beauty, mission and righteous superiority. The Christmas story proves this, for all who came to see the baby Jesus bowed to worship Him! **Are you too busy to stop to worship Him this Christmas? Is He the focus for your activity these days?** Read Luke 1:39-45 and see how John the Baptist, as a fetus, responded to the presence of Jesus when His mother Mary appeared. Make sure you bow down or leap for joy as well at some point during these days of Christmas.

## December 23: By The Spirit

*"How will this be," Mary asked the angel,*
*"since I am a virgin?" - Luke 1:34.*

Mary asked how God's will could possibly be accomplished in her life when the angel announced that she was pregnant and would give birth to Jesus. The angel's answer was simple: The Holy Spirit would achieve what the angel promised. The same is true for you and may be the only answer you also receive if you ask "how will this be?". Your purpose and God's will for your life will only be done with God's help and through His power. **Are you facing a huge purpose, intimidated by your own inadequacy to achieve it? Are you delaying in doing God's will because you don't understand how it will all work out?** Because you cannot see the end, are you refusing to even start? Read Genesis 22:1-19 and be encouraged to see how the Holy Spirit provided all Abraham needed when he set out to obey God and sacrifice his son.

## December 24: Wise Men

*"Where is the one who has been born king of the Jews?"*
*- Matthew 2:2.*

The Magi asked this question and Herod, the reigning king, was threatened by the presence of a rival king. But the wise men were looking for the baby to worship and give Him gifts. The responses are still the same today: Some are threatened by Jesus, but others recognize their need to worship the King of kings. **Are you searching for Jesus as the Magi did or are you intimidated by His desire to be Lord over all areas of your life?** Matthew 2:1-12 shows the price the Magi paid to seek out and worship the King; go pay the same price.

## December 25: Christmas Favor

*"But why am I so favored, that the mother of my Lord should come to me?" - Luke 1:43.*

Elizabeth saw herself as favored by God because Mary came to visit her while carrying Jesus in her womb. **How much more favored are you because Jesus has come to visit you personally in the presence and power of the Spirit? Do you see yourself as favored by God? Do you act like it? What should someone who is favored like you be doing? Pray? Worship? Do good deeds? Rejoice? Give thanks? Learn more about God and His ways?** Read about your position of favor in the Lord in Ephesians 1:15-23 and then meditate on the meaning and implications of the Christmas truth that God is with you. Merry Christmas!

## December 26: Potential

*"What then is this child going to be?" - Luke 1:66.*

The people marveled at the events surrounding John the Baptist's birth and knew he was destined to be special in the plan of God. Moses' parents looked at him and saw the same. **What do you see when you see others? Your own children and family members? Do you see their weaknesses and problems or what they can be in the will of God? And yourself? Do you see problems or do you see potential?** Read Acts 7:20 and ask God to help you see people as He does, so you can cooperate with His plan for their lives.

# December 27: Witnessing

*"How will you escape being condemned to hell?" - Matthew 23:33.*

There is only one way for people to escape hell, and that is to put their faith in Christ and then live life in the Spirit. And there is only one way people can find out about Christ, and that is when you and others like you tell them the good news. **What are you doing to spread the gospel? How much personal witnessing do you do? What do you do to support world missions?** As you approach a new year, give thought to this practice in your life as you read Romans 10:14-18.

# December 28: Press Through

*"And what does the Lord require of you?" - Micah 6:8.*

What God has put in your heart to do will not just magically occur. It will not be part of the heavenly Jerusalem which descends from heaven, but will require effort on your part, often more toil than you first thought. If you don't set it into a goal, however, it will remain a wish and go unfulfilled. **What is the Lord requiring you to do? What price are you ready to pay? What are your goals for the coming years of your life?** Read Philippians 3:12-14, and then determine what you need to press through to get to.

# December 29: Your Life

*"What concern is it of yours?" - John 21:22.*

You may invest a lot of energy worrying about or meddling in the affairs of someone else, just as Peter was doing when Jesus asked him today's question. That energy is better directed into your own work and world, and that involves knowing what Jesus wants you to do—His will for your life. **Are you wasting energy trying to live other's lives? Is this a defense mechanism to keep you from pursuing**

**God's plan for your life? What are the things that should concern you in the coming year?** Read Philippians 3:7-11 and notice how focused Paul was on his own life and work; that is how focused you should be with your life.

## December 30: Fickle

*"Was I fickle when I intended to do this?"*
*- 2 Corinthians 1:17.*

The dictionary definition of fickle is: "marked by lack of steadfastness, constancy, or stability; given to erratic changeableness." You will never accomplish anything for the Lord without learning how to set a goal and stick with it to the end (even though as in Paul's case in 2 Corinthians, he was unable to fulfill his stated goal). **What are the goals you are working on right now? What are your goals for the new year? If you are a good starter but poor finisher, why do you think that is? What are you afraid of that is preventing you from planning or following through?** Read Romans 15:23-29 and notice that Paul's success did not just happen; he gave it thought and had a plan. Follow Paul's example and develop a plan for your own life and work and then be diligent to carry it out.

## December 31: Stop Doing

*"If you do what is right, will you not be accepted?"*
*- Genesis 4:6.*

There are activities that are good and noble, but they are not right for you. You have a purpose and gifts that define what you should do and what you should not do. As you enter a new year, this is a good time to reflect on your world and where you are investing yourself. **What should you stop doing in the coming year? Of what do you need to do more? Where should you spend your time so your return on investment is at the maximum?** Read Acts 6:1-7, and notice that the apostles had to say "no" to important work, but the results were that more people were involved and the church grew. Now go apply the same principle to your own life's work.

# CONCLUSION

This was a fun project to work on over a year's time. It all started with a comment that someone made, "Quality questions lead to a quality life." Then I started by identifying all the questions I could find in the gospels and put them on my website. Then I had the idea to do a daily devotional featuring questions, knowing I did not have 366 to use when I started. So it was truly a faith project when I started.

From the gospels, I branched out to the epistles, then the Wisdom literature and finally to all of the Old Testament. I actually had more than the 366 I needed when it was all said and done, but the questions I used were the ones that most impressed me. The final touch of faith was to find a cross reference to another part of the Bible for each question, and to see if I could do that using all 66 books. Once again, my faith was rewarded and I was able to find what I needed, with the Lord's guiding hand leading me on.

One byproduct of this particular devotional is that I am using more questions in my own teaching. I have never been a particularly effective facilitator at times because I did not feel comfortable with silence when I asked a question while people thought and processed their answers. So I would keep talking and teaching, never allowing the 'pregnant silence' that would or could produce thoughtful responses. Now I almost hear the silence after Jesus asked His questions, while people thought and pondered what and whether or not to respond. I am using questions much more effectively after this writing this devotional, although I have a ways to go – I still don't like the silence.

One final product of this daily devotional is the change to my writing style. Since I endeavored to make these daily devotionals short, I had to improve my writing – or at least be more efficient. I also wanted to make each day's offering about the same size, which required me to get right to the point and not waste words. This has also made me a better writer, well, perhaps a more efficient writer, for the 'better' part is to be determined by the reader and not the writer in this case.

I share all this to help you with your own approach to writing and creativity. Both are always evolving into what they can be for each of us, and they are both art forms that should express your individuality – as this project does reflect mine. I am now 'addicted' to daily devotionals and will continue to write daily with the view toward 'shipping' what I write out each day. Then at the end of the year, I will publish my work for posterity to judge and hopefully enjoy. Of course, my ultimate purpose is to help people engage God's word every day, both to read it and then apply it.

So there you have the final thoughts on the project What Would Jesus Ask You Today? I hope you use it for the purposes for which it was written, and may God be glorified by this approach to His timeless Word. I would appreciate hearing from you as to what this study has one for you, or how you are using it for personal or group study. Finally, I pray you will look at this work and think, "I can do this or that" and then go and do it, producing your own work that reflects your personal values and God-given insight. As you do, I will keep writing and creating, pursuing the never-ending quest for writer's satisfaction and sense of accomplishment. Thank you and may God bless you in your own creative expressions.

# What Would Jesus Ask You Today?

# Scripture References

## Genesis



## Exodus



## Leviticus



## Numbers



## Deueteronomy



## Deueteronomy (cont.)



## Joshua



## Judges



## Ruth



## 1 Samuel



## 2 Samuel



## 1 Kings

## Matthew (cont.)



## Matthew

## Mark



## Mark (cont.)



## Luke

## Luke (cont.)



## Luke (cont.)

## Hebrews

| | |
|---|---|
| 1:1-4 | March 16 |
| 2:4-18 | May 22 |
| 3:15 | May 16 |
| 4:6-11 | March 25 |
| 4:14-17 | September 15 |
| 5:7-10 | April 17 |
| 5:11-6:3 | February 2 |
| 10:23-25 | February 15 |
| 10:24-25 | August 30 |
| 10:36-39 | September 16 |

## Hebrews (cont.)

| | |
|---|---|
| 11 | February 16 |
| 11:1-2 | February 12 |
| 11:6 | February 6 |
| 12:4-6 | September 11 |
| 12:7-12 | June 13 |
| 12:5 | October 7 |
| 12:14 | February 3 |
| 12:18-29 | November 10 |
| 12:25-29 | August 12 |
| 13:1-8 | September 19 |

## James

| | |
|---|---|
| 1:5-8 | January 5 |
| 1:16-18 | October 6 |
| 1:19-20 | June 1 |
| 2:1-13 | May 2 |
| 2:14-17 | June 24 |
| 2:20 | May 8 |
| 4:4 | January 19 |
| 4:5 | July 10 |

## 1 Peter

| | |
|---|---|
| 1:3-7 | March 2 |
| 3:8-17 | May 30 |
| 3:15 | May 27 |
| 4 | January 22 |
| 5:7 | April 25 |

## 2 Peter

| | |
|---|---|
| 1:5-8 | June 19 |
| 1:12-15 | October 25 |
| 1:19-21 | April 24 |
| 3 | October 7 |
| 3:9 | June 3 |
| 3:14-18 | July 30 |

## 1 John

| | |
|---|---|
| 1:8-10 | June 9 |
| 2:12-14 | April 30 |

## 1 John (cont.)

| | |
|---|---|
| 3:16-18 | March 24 |
| 4:18 | July 23 |
| 5:11-12 | November 19 |

## 2 John

| | |
|---|---|
| 1:1-6 | November 24 |

## 3 John

| | |
|---|---|
| 2 | March 6 |

## Jude

| | |
|---|---|
| 1:24-25 | November 26 |

## Revelation

| | |
|---|---|
| 7:7-17 | November 29 |
| 7:9-10 | September 26 |
| 10:1-4 | July 9 |
| 12 | September 21 |
| 12:11 | August 20 |

# About the Author

John Stanko was born in Pittsburgh, Pennsylvania. After graduating from St. Basil's Prep School in Stamford, Connecticut, he attended Duquesne University where he received his bachelor's and master's degrees in eco-nomics in 1972 and 1974 respectively.

Since then, John has served as an administrator, teacher, consultant, author, and pastor in his profession-al career. He holds a second master's degree in pastoral ministries, and earned his doctorate in pastoral minis-tries from Liberty Theological Seminary in Houston, Texas in 1995. He recently completed a second doctor of ministry degree at Reformed Presbyterian Theological Seminary in Pittsburgh.

John has taught extensively on the topics of time management, life purpose and organization, and has conducted leadership and purpose training sessions throughout the United States and in 32 countries. He is also certified to administer the DISC and other related personality assessments as well as the Natural Church Development profile for churches. In 2006, he earned the privilege to facilitate for The Pacific Institute of Seattle, a leadership and personal development program, and for The Leadership Circle, a provider of cultural and executive 360-degree profiles. He has authored fifteen books and written for many publications around the world.

John founded a personal and leadership develop-ment company, called PurposeQuest, in 2001 and today travels the world to speak, consult and inspire leaders and people everywhere. From 2001-2008, he spent six months a year in Africa and still enjoys visiting and working on that continent, while teaching for Geneva College's Masters of Organizational Leadership and the Center for Urban Biblical Ministry in his hometown of Pittsburgh, Pennsylvania. John has been married for 44 years to Kathryn Scimone Stanko, and they have two adult children and two grandchildren. In 2009, John was appointed the administrative pastor for discipleship at Allegheny Center Alliance Church on the North Side of Pittsburgh where he served for five years. Most re-cently, John founded Urban Press, a publishing service designed to tell stories of the city, from the city, and to the city.

# Keep in Touch with John W. Stanko

www.purposequest.com
www.johnstanko.us
www.stankobiblestudy.com
www.stankomondaymemo.com

or via email at johnstanko@gmail.com

John also does extensive relief and community development work in Kenya. You can see some of his projects at www.purposequest.com/contributions

PurposeQuest International
PO Box 8882
Pittsburgh, PA 15221-0882

## Additional Titles by John W. Stanko

A Daily Dose of Proverbs
A Daily Taste of Proverbs
Changing the Way We Do Church
I Wrote This Book on Purpose
Life Is A Gold Mine: Can You Dig It?
Strictly Business
The Faith Files, Volume 1
The Faith Files, Volume 2
The Faith Files, Volume 3
The Leadership Walk
The Price of Leadership
Unlocking the Power of Your Creativity
Unlocking the Power of Your Productivity Unlocking the Power of Your Purpose
Unlocking the Power of You
What Would Jesus Ask You Today?
Your Life Matters

Live the Word Commentary: Matthew
Live the Word Commentary: Mark
Live the Word Commentary: Luke
Live the Word Commentary: John
Live the Word Commentary: Acts
Live the Word Commentary: Romans
Live the Word Commentary: 1 & 2 Corinthians
Live the Word Commentary: Galatians, Ephesians, Philippians, Colossians, Philemon
Live the Word Commentary: Hebrews
Live the Word Commentary: Revelation

www.ingramcontent.com/pod-product-compliance
Lightning Source LLC
Chambersburg PA
CBHW072000040426
42447CB00009B/1418
*9781633600157*